Best Hikes Near
Boston

STEVE MIRSKY

FALCONGUIDES

GUILFORD, CONNECTICUT
HELENA, MONTANA

AN IMPRINT OF GLOBE PEQUOT PRESS

This book is dedicated to countless volunteers who maintain many miles on the routes covered within these chapters. It is their selflessness that makes enjoyable hiking possible.

To buy books in quantity for corporate use or incentives, call **(800) 962–0973** or e-mail **premiums@GlobePequot.com**.

FALCONGUIDES®

Copyright © 2011 by Morris Book Publishing, LLC

FalconGuides is an imprint of Globe Pequot Press.
Falcon, FalconGuides, and Outfit Your Mind are registered trademarks of Morris Book Publishing, LLC.

Interior photos: Steve Mirsky unless otherwise credited
Text design: Sheryl P. Kober
Project editor: Julie Marsh
Layout artist: Maggie Peterson

Maps: Hartdale Maps © Morris Book Publishing, LLC
GPS coordinates supplied by Melissa Baker and Daniel Lloyd

Library of Congress Cataloging-in-Publication Data

Mirsky, Steve, 1972-
  Best hikes near Boston / Steve Mirsky.
    p. cm.
  ISBN 978-0-7627-6091-6
1. Hiking—Massachusetts—Boston Region—Guidebooks. 2. Trails—Massachusetts—Boston Region—Guidebooks. 3. Boston Region (Mass.)—Guidebooks. I. Title.
  GV199.42.M42B676 2011
  917.44—dc22
                                                                    2010050794

Printed in the United States of America
10 9 8 7 6 5 4 3 2 1

Contents

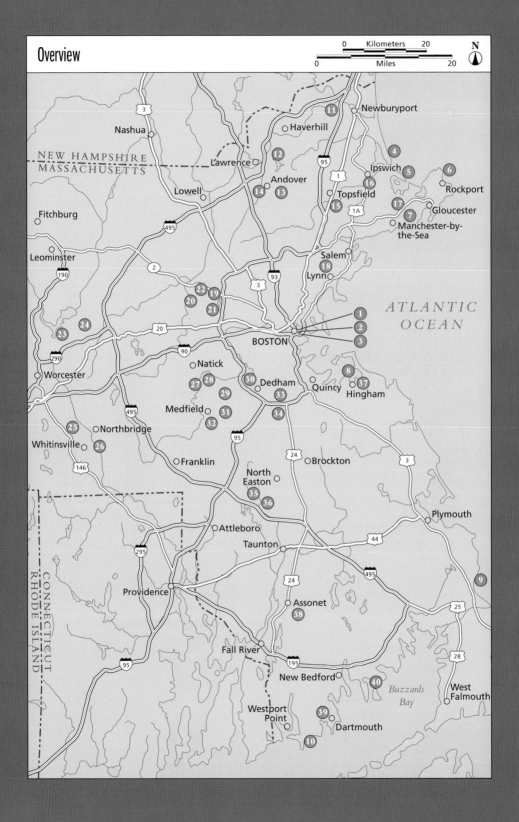

0   Kilometers   20

0   Miles   20

N

NEW HAMPSHIRE
MASSACHUSETTS

Nashua

Haverhill

11 Newburyport

Lawrence

12

4

Andover

14

13

Ipswich

5

6

Rockport

Lowell

95

1

16

Topsfield

15

1A

17

7

Gloucester

Manchester-by-
the-Sea

Fitchburg

2

Salem

Leominster

190

93

3

18

Lynn

ATLANTIC
OCEAN

22 19
20
21

24

23

20

290

90

BOSTON

1

2

3

Worcester

Natick

8

37

27 28

30 Dedham

Quincy

Hingham

29

33

Medfield

31

34

32

495

25

Northbridge

95

Brockton

3

26

Whitinsville

24

146

Franklin

North
Easton

35

36

Plymouth

Attleboro

44

295

Taunton

24

495

9

Providence

Assonet

38

25

CONNECTICUT
RHODE ISLAND

Fall River

195

28

New Bedford

40

Buzzards
Bay

95

West
Falmouth

Westport
Point

39

Dartmouth

10

Acknowledgments

I am indebted to the countless volunteers who maintain trails throughout the Boston Metropolitan Area and the State of Massachusetts, whether it is the extensive Bay Circuit Trail, skirting the boundaries of Boston from North Shore to South Shore or the smaller municipally owned preserves that depend on private donations to remain open to visitors. Their efforts, along with individuals who have had the foresight to preserve open space even in the face of extreme development pressures, make many routes in this guide book possible.

I am also grateful to the many individuals I encountered out on the trails who shared both their love of the outdoors and their familiarity with some of the following routes that I hiked throughout the Boston area. Most fellow hikers I encountered went out of their way to offer advice as to which portions of the route were better for experiencing views, or which sections of trail were best to avoid due to weather conditions.

Thanks to the expert team of editors and production staff at Globe Pequot Press for helping me make this guide the best it can be. Special thanks to my wife, Renee, who supported my time away on weekends to cover these hikes and my extended periods buried behind my laptop typing up these chapters.

The site of Walden Pond, made famous by Henry David Thoreau (hike 20)

Introduction

Not only is Boston a world-class city literally studded with historical landmarks like those on the Freedom Trail as well as Bunker Hill and Faneuil Hall, but the metropolitan area as well as all of eastern Massachusetts is peppered with obvious monuments to the past, and less apparent treasures lie just around the corner where you least expect them. As you embark on the hikes contained within these chapters, you'll get up close and personal with must-see destinations like Walden Pond, where Henry Thoreau popularized rugged individualism as a defining American attribute; Minute Man National Historic Park's Battle Road, where the original roadbed used by advancing redcoats and Paul Revere's freedom riders is still intact and open for exploration; and the Blackstone Canal River Valley Heritage Corridor, a dynamic symbol of the Industrial Revolution's dawning where the remarkably straight-cut stone blocks lining the canal's locks sit seemingly just as intact as the day they were placed there by horse and by backbreaking manual labor.

Of course no place is without history, but in Massachusetts, place and history are synonymous. Farther afield on less publicized routes, you'll find that it's simply impossible to lose yourself in the woods without being confronted with at least a little bit of curious history. On all of these routes, there's a palpable sense that history was in the making at some point, ranging from a rough stone foundation covered by underbrush to a well-preserved nationally recognized historic site. Digging a little deeper, for instance, you'll find that offshore near Nasketucket Bay State Reservation, Herman Melville set sail on the whaling ship *Acushnet* from Fairhaven and later described what he experienced in *Moby-Dick;* that Judge Samuel Sewall of Salem witch trials infamy got stranded on a sandbar off Plum Island's Sandy Point in the 1600s and wrote of it in his journal; or that within the forest of Lynn Woods, a remarkably well-preserved patch of wilderness right in the middle of thick urban development, Hester Prynne surreptitiously met Mr. Dimmesdale for a secret meeting in Nathaniel Hawthorne's novel *The Scarlet Letter.* It's this juxtaposition between wide-open spaces, rich history dating back to the birth of a nation, and the relentless march of pressures associated with a highly dense and ever-burgeoning population that make exploring the Boston area's patches of nature so intriguing.

Boston Weather

Located near sea level, the Boston area boasts attractive hiking year-round. Even though the ocean moderates the climate here in comparison to interior Northern New England locations, there are still periods of unpredictability that is synonymous with weather patterns in the Northeast. Since Boston area weather varies greatly depending on the season, winter temperatures can dip below zero aided by a wind chill during a handful of days but the average between December and February is 30°F while June through August typically average in the 70s. Periods of humidity during the summer can spike to uncomfortable levels without warning, while winter precipitation can range from freezing rain to snow within the same day. Because of this relative unpredictability, trail conditions can change greatly from day to day. However, you will be well prepared with the following rule of thumb: Layer up in winter with a breathable long-sleeved shirt, a polar fleece pullover, and a waterproof coat for the outer layer. Depending on whether trails are covered with deep or packed snow or ice, either waterproof boots with gaiters and snowshoes or waterproof hiking boots outfitted with ice grippers will serve you well. Spring (March through May) tends to be wet, muddy at times, and increasingly buggy beginning in April. Wear your bug repellent, breathable T-shirt, sweatshirt, and windbreaker with waterproof hiking boots. In summer (June through August), a T-shirt, long pants tucked into socks, liberally applied insect repellent, and plenty of water will keep you comfortable. My favorite hiking season is fall (September through November). The mosquitoes and gnats are gone, foliage is starting to turn colors, and stretches of blue skies with warm, bright sun and cool breezes make hiking a joy. The only downside is that thousands of others likely feel the same way, so you are guaranteed company en route.

Boston skyline views from atop Wilson Mountain (hike 30)

However, once you get beyond exclusively focusing on personal comfort as the determining factor of when to hit the trails, you'll be rewarded with rich experiences that are unique to particular seasons. Sure, January's icy winds may have you wincing and initially shivering, but if you're bundled up properly, there's simply no better time to strap on your cross-country skis and glide over a slight decline on a wide-open wood road through snow-covered hemlock groves. And in early June, just as newly hatched and energized clouds of mosquitoes and gnats relentlessly encircle your head, tons of delicate bulbous-blossomed pink lady slippers seemingly sprout in every direction on the forest floor, making your perseverance well worthwhile.

Weather Averages for Boston

Month	Avg. High	Avg. Low	Mean	Avg. Precip	Record High	Record Low
Jan	36°F	22°F	29°F	3.92 in.	72°F (1950)	-30°F (1946)
Feb	39°F	24°F	32°F	3.30 in.	70°F (1985)	-18°F (1934)
Mar	46°F	31°F	39°F	3.85 in.	89°F (1998)	-8°F (1872)
Apr	56°F	41°F	48°F	3.60 in.	94°F (1976)	11°F (1874)
May	67°F	50°F	59°F	3.24 in.	97°F (1880)	31°F (1882)
Jun	77°F	59°F	68°F	3.22 in.	100°F (1952)	41°F (1945)
Jul	82°F	65°F	74°F	3.06 in.	104°F (1911)	50°F (1988)
Aug	80°F	64°F	72°F	3.37 in.	102°F (1975)	46°F (1940)
Sep	73°F	57°F	65°F	3.47 in.	102°F (1881)	34°F (1914)
Oct	62°F	46°F	54°F	3.79 in.	90°F (1963)	25°F (1936)
Nov	52°F	38°F	45°F	3.98 in.	83°F (1950)	−2°F (1875)
Dec	42°F	28°F	35°F	3.73 in.	76°F (1998)	−17°F (1933)

(Statistics from the Weather Channel, August 14, 2010)

Flora and Fauna

While on the trails covered in this book, you'll encounter mostly benign creatures such as deer, squirrels, chipmunks, wild turkeys, and a variety of songbirds and shorebirds. More rarely seen (during the daylight hours especially) are coyotes, raccoons, and opossums. Deer in some of the parks are remarkably tame and may linger on or close to the trail as you approach.

While rare, the Boston area's preserves and parks may also be habitat for black bear, copperheads, and rattlesnakes. Encounters are infrequent, but you should be prepared to react properly if you run across a venomous snake, bear, or rabid nocturnal animal such as a raccoon or opossum. Snakes generally only strike if they are threatened. You are too big to be dinner, so they typically avoid contact with humans. Keep your distance and they will keep theirs. If you come across a bear, make yourself as big as possible and do not run. If you don't act like or look like prey, you stand a good chance of not being attacked. Warning them ahead of time by wearing a bell helps to avoid contact in the first place. And if you see an animal normally seen at night with matted fur and foam on its mouth, steer clear of it. If necessary, turn back and postpone your hike. Rabid animals can't be reasoned with and should never be approached or fed. It's not worth risking personal safety for a planned hike. Chances are that another route covered in this guidebook is not more than a half hour away.

Leave No Trace and Trail Etiquette

Even though a trail surface appears rugged and impervious to erosion, all walking surfaces in the forest consist of fragile landscapes that may take a century or more to recover from damage. Even though it is not always readily apparent, many trails in the highly populated Boston area are heavily used year-round. Out of courtesy for future hiking enjoyment and in order to perpetuate a healthy sustainable ecosystem, we as trail users and advocates must be especially vigilant to make sure our passage leaves no lasting mark. Here are some basic guidelines for preserving trails in the region:

- Pack out all your own trash, including biodegradable items like orange peels. You might also pack out garbage left by less considerate hikers.
- Don't approach or feed any wild creatures—the ground squirrel eyeing your snack food is best able to survive if it remains self-reliant.
- Don't pick wildflowers or gather rocks, antlers, feathers, and other treasures along the trail. Removing these items will only take away from the next hiker's experience.
- Avoid damaging trailside soils and plants by remaining on the established route. This is also a good rule of thumb for avoiding poison oak and ivy.
- Don't cut switchbacks, which can promote erosion.
- Be courteous by not making loud noises while hiking.
- Some of these trails are multiuse, which means you'll share them with other hikers, trail runners, mountain bikers, and possibly equestrians. Familiarize yourself with the proper trail etiquette, yielding the trail when appropriate.
- Use outhouses at trailheads or along the trail.

Beyond preserving the natural environment, being considerate of fellow hikers and following trail etiquette ensure that all trail users have the opportunity to enjoy these natural treasures. Each one of us has our own ideas about what makes a trail excursion most memorable and refreshing. Some prefer the company of friends and family for some much-needed bonding time in the "wide open." Others prefer to hike in solitude and drink in the atmosphere untouched as much as possible by human society. And still others, where permissible, like to add another dimension of horseback riding or mountain biking to the outdoor experience. The key is to be mindful and respectful of others on the trail. What may simply be an act of calling out for your dog that has strayed or shouting ahead for your children may be a major annoyance for a fellow hiker nearby who is bird-watching or doing some natural landscape sketching trailside. Perhaps you love horses and can't imagine why others would perceive them as anything other than gentle giants. That is until you walk in the wake of your trusty steed without keeping your eye to the ground. A little common sense and compromise go a long way toward peacefully accommodating everybody's right, within the parameters of posted park or trail-use rules, to enjoy the trails in their own way at the moment.

Here are some general rules of thumb in the absence of trail rules that are usually posted on a signboard at many trailheads:

If pets are permitted on the trails, please keep them leashed so they do not disturb other trail users or local wildlife. Pick up after your pet not only for aesthetic reasons but also to mitigate polluting the nearby surface water.

Since forest trails don't come with traffic signals and signage, a rough protocol between trail users should be observed. Bicyclists should yield to equestrians, runners, and hikers, keeping their bikes under control and at a safe speed. Runners and hikers should yield to equestrians. Downhill traffic should yield to uphill traffic, and be sure to warn people when you are planning to pass. Use your voice to warn equestrians, not bells or horns, as these may frighten horses. Just to be safe, move off the trail when a horse approaches.

Log bench overlooking Broadmoor Wildlife Sanctuary marsh (hike 28)

Leave the trail bed and surrounding forest floor as you found them or better by packing out your trash and disposing of it properly. The most effective and convenient method of dealing with refuse is to remove food from its packaging before you leave home and put it into ziplock bags. This way, the litter you'll need to pack out will be minimal and the ziplock bags can serve as sealed waste bags for organic waste such as apple cores and banana peels. Remember that even discarding organic biodegradables onto the forest floor is more than unsightly. It inadvertently feeds wildlife, which will come to depend on this artificial food source.

Enjoy observing wildlife from a respectful distance. You may wish to pack a camera, binoculars, or sketchbook to record your observations. Stalking or harassing any form of wildlife, whether it is a lone salamander or a grazing herd of deer, not only ruins the chance of future hikers being able to experience the same sighting but also disrupts the animals' mating and feeding patterns. Humans already inflict enough disruption, such as road and home building and water usage, on the natural environment as a normal course of daily living. Make it a point to go out of your way to treat these preserves and parks as a refuge from human encroachment, allowing wildlife to enjoy their habitat.

Treat hikes with children as both an adventure and an opportunity to instill an appreciation for the environment. Pack a nature guide to help them learn about the features and creatures in the world around them. When planning a trek with children, consider the difficulty in distance and terrain so that it matches their interests and stamina. Encourage children with extra snacks to keep up their energy levels and remember to pack tissue for their personal hygiene. The familiar phrase "take nothing but pictures and leave nothing but footprints" is a simple but powerful way to teach children the importance of treading lightly on the land. After all, as they say in real estate circles, "Land, they aren't making any more of it."

Maximize Hiking Enjoyment

Nearly all of the trails profiled in this guide are within an hour's drive, or a little more, from downtown Boston, minus traffic of course. As you may imagine, weekends or late-morning to mid-afternoon during weekdays present the best times for automobile travel. Best times for trail use depend on the weather and people's schedule. Of course the closer you are to the city, the greater chance that you will have ample company on the trails. Keep these factors in mind when choosing a hiking destination.

In many cases, a little advance planning and preparation will go a long way toward making your hike more enjoyable. While many trails listed in this guide are easily accessible and require light to moderate endurance, some simple preparation will ensure maximum enjoyment and allow you to walk away with fond memories. It only takes a simple twist of the ankle to turn an otherwise brisk afternoon hike into a grueling and painful ordeal possibly extending into the night until being discovered and assisted. Of course emergencies don't distinguish between the unprepared and highly seasoned among us, but with the proper physical conditioning, appropriate footwear, ample water, a survival kit, and some energy food, you can keep the odds very much in your favor that injury won't strike. Even if you do find yourself compromised, what would otherwise end up resulting in hours of pain and misery could instead be a moderate inconvenience.

Getting in shape. Good physical conditioning and stamina are essential for enjoying a hike of more than a few miles. Prepare with regular walking around your home or at work for comparable distances. Before you tackle the rocky ridges and steep climbs that characterize many of these routes, begin by taking the stairs at work, or finding hills in your neighborhood to climb. You may also wish to join a gym where you might supplement your conditioning program with work on treadmills and stair-climbing equipment. Remember that when planning a group outing, consider the condition and stamina of the weakest member in your party when choosing your destination.

Basic first aid. Hiking in the Boston area is generally safe. Still, you should know the basics of first aid, including how to treat bleeding, bites and stings, and fractures, strains, or sprains. No matter how well prepared you are, unless you're a trained medical technician who deals with medical emergencies on a regular basis, witnessing or experiencing a sudden injury clouds your ability to react quickly and effectively. Having the right tools and a few basic rehearsals covering some common injuries make a big impact on whether you're able to help yourself or others effectively in a timely fashion. Here are some basics to get you started:

- While nearly all of the hikes profiled in this book are close to population centers, it is a good idea to pack a basic first-aid kit on each excursion. Some supplies to consider include extra insect repellent for pesky mosquitoes and gnats, cleansing wipes, adhesive bandages, antibiotic ointment for cuts and scrapes, an elastic wrap for sprains and strains, moleskin to cover blisters, antihistamine tablets for allergic reactions to insect bites or stings, tweezers to remove splinters, sunscreen (SPF 15 or higher), and aspirin or acetaminophen for pain.

- Familiarize yourself with the symptoms of heat exhaustion, heat stroke, and hypothermia. Heat exhaustion symptoms include heavy sweating, muscle cramps, headache, dizziness, and fainting. Should you or any of your hiking party exhibit any of these symptoms, cool the victim down immediately by rehydrating and getting him or her to an air-conditioned location. Cold showers also help reduce body temperature. Heat stroke is much more serious: The victim may lose consciousness and the skin is hot and dry to the touch. In this event, call 911 immediately. Hypothermia does not require exposure to subzero temperatures. Even damp, relatively mild weather can make you susceptible, namely any condition that brings your body temperature below 95°F. Symptoms include uncontrollable shivering, confusion, and pale, cold skin. Treatment of mild symptoms begins with removing any wet clothing and replacing with dry layers, drinking hot liquids followed by eating a high-sugared snack, and maintaining movement to maximize blood flow. If conditions worsen, seek medical help immediately.

- Regardless of the weather, your body needs a lot of water while hiking. A full 32-ounce bottle is the minimum for these short hikes, but more is always better. Bring a full water bottle, whether water is available along the trail or not.
- Don't drink from streams, rivers, creeks, or lakes without treating or filtering the water first. Waterways and water bodies may host a variety of contaminants including bacteria, which can cause serious intestinal unrest.
- Prepare for extremes of both heat and cold by dressing in layers.
- Carry a backpack in which you can store extra clothing, ample drinking water and food, and whatever goodies, like guidebooks, cameras, and binoculars, you might want.
- Some area trails have cell phone coverage. Bring your device, but make sure it's turned off or on the vibrate setting while hiking. There's nothing like a "wake the dead"-loud ring to startle every creature, including fellow hikers.

Downtown Boston on the Freedom Trail (hike 1)

- Keep children under careful watch. Hazards along some of the trails include poison oak and ivy, uneven footing, and steep drop-offs; make sure children don't stray from the designated route. Children should carry a plastic whistle; if they become lost, they should stay in one place and blow the whistle to summon help.

Clothing. Weather in the Boston area varies greatly between the height of summer and the dead of winter. August humidity can be extremely oppressive while icy winter wind gusts can initiate frostbite within a matter of minutes. However, dressing accordingly will allow you to enjoy the benefits of hiking and the widely varied scenery year-round. Hot and humid summer days call for breathable fabrics that wick moisture away from your body, a hat, and sunscreen; layering warm clothing and outerwear can take the chill out of a winter hike. Weather may change quickly, especially in summer when surface heating might spawn pop-up thunderstorms, so it is always a good idea to stuff a windbreaker or rain jacket in your pack. Children often need to be reminded to add a layer as their bodies are affected by the weather more quickly than adults, so be certain that they have the proper clothing for the trek.

Footwear. While heavy-duty hiking boots are certainly suitable for the moderate-distance hikes profiled in the guide, you may be just as happy with lightweight, all-terrain walking shoes with solid, lug-type soles. There are a wide variety of styles and brands from which to choose, so you may wish to visit a local outdoor equipment retailer to find a pair that fit both your feet and your budget. Also, don't forget to include a pair of good quality hiking socks to go along with your shoes.

Food and water. For even a short hike, it is a good idea to pack high-energy snacks and extra water. On the hottest summer or coldest winter days, hydration and a quick energy boost may be just what are needed to assure an enjoyable trek. If you are hiking with children or pets, consider their needs as well when packing supplies for the hike.

Personal safety. Be alert to your surroundings; carry a whistle and/or pepper spray and a cell phone. If you observe people acting suspiciously or feel threatened, do not hesitate to leave the area and use a cell phone to call 911 for assistance. Most of the profiled hiking trails are within cell phone coverage areas. Let family and friends know your plans. Provide information on where you are going and when you expect to return. Hiking with a companion or group provides the safety of numbers. This is a great way to share your experience and learn from others.

Getting to the Trail

Nearly all the trails in this guide are convenient to main thoroughfares and major interstate highways that course through eastern Massachusetts. Each chapter provides detailed directions from highways to the trailhead. A street level map or atlas (available from retailers, printed from a software program like DeLorme's Street Atlas or TOPO USA, or downloaded from an Internet source such as Google Maps or MapQuest) will supplement the printed directions or help you find alternatives in the event of a traffic delay. With Boston's traffic congestion, you may wish to select your hikes based on day of the week, the time you have available, traffic conditions, and travel distance to the trailhead.

Using Map, Compass, and Global Positioning System (GPS) Devices
All of the trails described in this guide are well maintained, and most are marked or blazed. Following the included map will keep you on the right path, or you may choose a more detailed topographical map available from an outdoor equipment retailer, on various software programs, or online from the U.S. Geological Survey (www.usgs.gov). You may also wish to carry a compass or GPS device to enhance your skills with these navigation tools. Using all three in combination is an excellent way to check your current location and your direction of travel, as well as the terrain around you and ahead.

You may also be interested in improving your skills by joining a group that turns navigation into adventures. Geocaching is a scavenger hunt gone high-tech. Individuals or groups have hidden caches (usually a small waterproof container with a logbook and some small rewards) in parks and public places around the world. They share the GPS coordinates for the cache and invite others to find them. Once found, the individual is usually asked to sign the log, take a reward, and leave something in the box for the next searcher. Geocaching is a great way to improve skills with GPS devices, and many of the parks and trails listed in this guide contain geocaches. To learn more, visit www.geocaching.com.

How to Use This Guide

Each of the forty routes covered in *Best Hikes Near Boston* begins with a hike summary aiding in quick decision making. You'll learn about the trail terrain and what surprises the route has to offer. Next you'll find the quick, nitty-gritty details of the hike such as where the trailhead is located, hike length, approximate hiking time, difficulty rating, type of trail surface, other trail users, canine compatibility, land status, fees and permits, trail hours, map resources, trail contacts, and other information that will help you on your trek.

The **Finding the trailhead** section gives you dependable directions from a major route down to where you'll want to park your car. **The Hike** description is the meat of the chapter. Detailed and honest, it's a carefully researched impression of the trail. While it's impossible to cover everything, you can rest assured that we've been careful not to miss examining what's immediately apparent.

Approximate hiking times are based on the assumption that on flat ground, most walkers average 2 miles per hour. Adjust that rate by the steepness of the terrain and your level of fitness. Subtract time if you're an accomplished triathlete or add time if you're hiking with your kids, and you have a ballpark hiking duration. Be sure to add more time if you plan to picnic or take part in other activities like bird watching or photography.

In the **Miles and Directions** section, mileage cues identify all turns and trail name changes as well as points of interest.

All hikes in this book are ranked by **difficulty,** and most in this book range from easy to moderate. Some are more challenging due to increased distance and/or periods of sustained climbing. Remember that easy is a relative term. Some would argue that no hike involving any kind of climbing is easy, but here in the Boston area, hills are everywhere although not usually prolonged. To aid in the selection of a hike that suits particular needs and abilities, each is rated easy, moderate, or strenuous. Bear in mind that even the most challenging routes can be made easy by hiking within your limits and taking rests when you need them.

Easy hikes are generally short and flat, taking no longer than an hour to complete.

Moderate hikes involve increased distance and relatively mild changes in elevation, and will take one to two hours to complete.

Strenuous hikes feature some steep stretches, greater distances, and generally take longer than two hours to complete.

These are completely subjective ratings—consider that what you think is easy is entirely dependent on your level of fitness and the adequacy of your gear (primarily shoes). If you are hiking with a group, you should select a hike with a rating that's appropriate for the least fit and prepared in your party.

Trail Finder

Hike No.	Hike Name	Best Hikes for Families and Children	Best Hikes for Great Views	Best Hikes for Lake Lovers	Best Hikes for River Lovers	Best Hikes for Canyons	Best Hikes for Geology Lovers	Best Hikes for History Lovers	Best Hikes for Nature Lovers and Bird Watchers	Best Hikes for Dogs	Best Hikes for Physically Challanged
1	The Freedom Trail	●						●			●
2	Charles River Loop		●		●			●			●
3	Back Bay Fens: Isabella's Loop	●			●						●
4	Plum Island: Sandy Point Loop		●						●		
5	Crane Beach: Dune Loop	●	●						●		
6	Halibut Point Reservation		●			●	●				●
7	Coolidge Reservation	●	●								
8	World's End Reservation	●	●						●		
9	Ellisville Harbor State Park	●	●						●	●	
10	Horseneck Beach	●	●					●	●	●	●
11	Maudslay State Park	●	●		●				●	●	●
12	Weir Hill Reservation		●	●						●	
13	Skug River Loop								●		
14	Ward Reservation		●						●		
15	Ipswich River Wildlife Sanctuary	●	●						●		●
16	Appleton Farms Grass Rides	●						●			
17	Ravenswood Park	●					●		●		
18	Lynn Woods Reservation		●						●	●	
19	Minute Man Park: Battle Road Trail							●			
20	Walden Pond			●				●			

Trail Finder

Hike No.	Hike Name	Best Hikes for Families and Children	Best Hikes for Great Views	Best Hikes for Lake Lovers	Best Hikes for River Lovers	Best Hikes for Canyons	Best Hikes for Geology Lovers	Best Hikes for History Lovers	Best Hikes for Nature Lovers and Bird Watchers	Best Hikes for Dogs	Best Hikes for Physically Challenged
21	Mount Misery Loop								●	●	
22	Sandy Pond Loop			●							
23	Wachusett Reservoir			●					●		
24	Mount Pisgah Conservation Area	●									
25	Purgatory Chasm State Reservationi	●	●			●	●				
26	Blackstone River and Canal State Park				●			●			
27	Rocky Narrows Preserve		●		●	●			●		
28	Broadmoor Wildlife Sanctuary	●							●		
29	Noanet Woodlands			●				●			
30	Wilson Mountain Reservation	●	●	●					●		
31	Rocky Woods Reservation								●	●	●
32	Noon Hill Reservation								●	●	
33	Blue Hills Reservation: Great Blue Hill		●						●		
34	Blue Hills Reservation: Ponkapoag Pond	●		●					●	●	●
35	Borderland State Park	●		●					●	●	●
36	Wheaton Farm Conservation Area	●							●	●	
37	Whitney and Thayer Woods						●		●	●	
38	Freetown–Fall River State Forest				●				●	●	
39	Destruction Brook Woods Preserve							●	●	●	
40	Nasketucket Bay State Reservation								●	●	

Map Legend

TRANSPORTATION

- Freeway/Interstate Highway (90)
- U.S. Highway (24)
- State Highway (2)
- Unpaved Road
- Railroad

TRAILS

- Selected Route
- Trail or Fire Road
- Direction of Travel

WATER FEATURES

- Body of Water
- River or Creek
- Wetland or Meadow

LAND FEATURES

- Local & State Parks
- National Forest & Wilderness Areas
- Sand Area
- Tidal Flat

SYMBOLS

- (20) Trailhead
- Bridge
- Building/Point of Interest
- Campground
- Gate
- Interpretive Panel
- Mountain/Peak
- P Parking
- × Physical Feature—Small
- Picnic Area
- Restroom
- Scenic View
- ○ Towns and Cities
- === Tunnel

Views of Cambridge across the Charles River (hike 3)

A recreational lifeline for Bostonians seeking respite from city life.

The Freedom Trail

You'd certainly be hard-pressed to find a more iconic urban hike than Boston's Freedom Trail. If you have the time to explore all the historic sites along this route, you can easily spend an entire day, but perhaps a weekend is more realistic if you want the full experience of stopping for lunch at one of the many authentic Italian restaurants in the North End and exploring the Charles River waterfront surrounding the USS Constitution, aka Old Ironsides.

Start: Begin following the red painted line from the visitor center entrance in Boston Common

Nearest town: Boston

Distance: 2.9 miles one way

Approximate hiking time: 2.5 hours (all day if visiting sights)

Difficulty: Easy

Trail surface: Concrete, asphalt, and cobblestone

Seasons: Year-round

Other trail users: Shoppers, diners, sightseers

Canine compatibility: Dogs on leash per city ordinance

Land status: Freedom Trail Foundation

Fees and permits: None

Schedule: Sunrise to sunset daily

Maps: Available in the visitor center and at www.the freedomtrail.org/maps/pdfs /boston-nps-map.pdf

Trail contacts: The Freedom Trail Foundation, 99 Chauncy Street, Suite 401, Boston, MA 02111, (617) 357-8300; info@thefree domtrail.org

Finding the trailhead: From the Boyleston T Station, walk up through Boston Common paralleling Tremont Street to your right. GPS: N42 21.039/W71 3.870

From the Boyleston T Station at Boston Common, walk up alongside Tremont Street to the visitor center off to your left. Here you can arrange a formal albeit playfully irreverent tour with expert guides dressed in period costumes. If you decide on this approach, you won't be covering the entire route or be in need of these directions, but if you want to fully explore the Freedom Trail on your own, read on.

Begin from the visitor center entrance following a red painted line, which either continues or transitions into a thick row of red brick embedded into the sidewalks and roadbeds outlining the route. The red line may be broken in spots but provides a fairly carefree outline of where to proceed from beginning to end. After strolling through Boston Common, you'll climb a set of stairs to the front of the Massachusetts State House across Beacon Street. The first cornerstone was laid in 1796 under the direction of Acting Governor Samuel Adams, with Paul Revere officiating.

Continue by heading back down the hill on Park Street, now paralleling the Common to your right. There is no red line on this street, but upon returning to Tremont Street and turning left, you will be following a redbrick line. You'll pass the Granary Burying Ground to your left almost immediately upon making this turn. Here lie ancient headstones of greats like John Hancock and five victims of the Boston Massacre.

Rigging on the USS *Constitution,* the northern end of the Freedom Trail

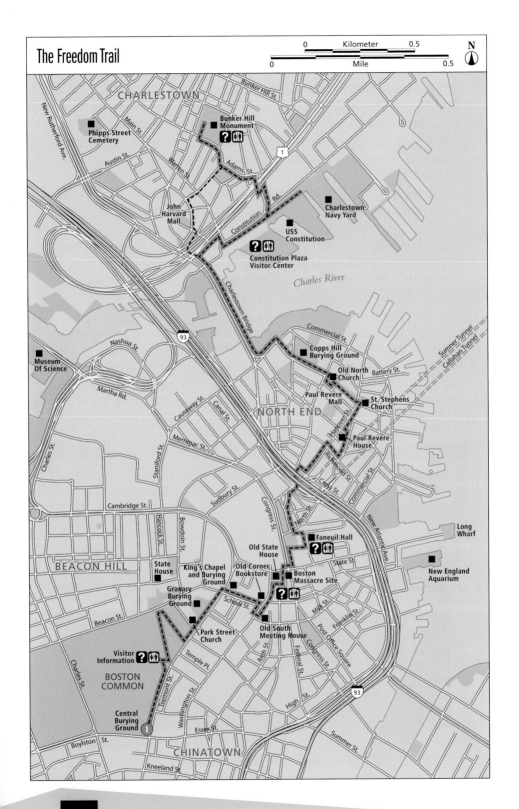

The Freedom Trail

0 Kilometer 0.5
0 Mile 0.5

N

CHARLESTOWN

Phipps Street Cemetery
Bunker Hill Monument
New Rutherford Ave.
Main St.
Warren St.
Austin St.
Adams St.
John Harvard Mall
Constitution Rd.
1
Charlestown Navy Yard
USS Constitution
Constitution Plaza Visitor Center
Charlestown Bridge
Charles River

93
Nashua St.
Museum Of Science
Martha Rd.
Commercial St.
Copps Hill Burying Ground
Sumner Tunnel
Callahan Tunnel
Old North Church
Battery St.
Paul Revere Mall
St. Stephens Church
NORTH END
Hanover St.
Paul Revere House
Richmond St.
Cross St.

Charles St.
Causeway St.
Canal St.
Merrimac St.
Staniford St.
Sudbury St.
Cambridge St.
Hancock St.
Bowdoin St.
Congress St.
North St.

BEACON HILL
State House
King's Chapel and Burying Ground
Old Corner Bookstore
Faneuil Hall
State St.
Long Wharf
New England Aquarium
New Atlantic Ave.
Old State House
Boston Massacre Site
Gramary Burying Ground
School St.
Milk St.
Post Office Square
Franklin St.
Beacon St.
Park Street Church
Old South Meeting House
Congress St.
Federal St.
93

Visitor Information
Temple Pl.
Tremont St.
Washington St.
Arch St.
High St.

BOSTON COMMON

Central Burying Ground
1
Essex St.
Summer St.
Boylston St.
Kneeland St.

CHINATOWN

You'll soon have another encounter with the departed at the King's Chapel and Burying Ground, Boston's oldest cemetery established in 1688. The headstones of luminaries like Governor John Winthrop still maintain their ornate carvings of scenes like skeletons brandishing swords at the Grim Reaper. On the corner of School and Washington Streets, you'll pass a group of interesting metallic sculptures in front of Border's Bookstore before crossing Washington Street to the Old South Meeting House. It was here in 1773 that 7,000 angry citizens gathered to protest the Tea Act imposed by England.

Be sure to pay a visit to the brick Old State House Museum to your left before crossing State Street and heading down Congress Street. Turn right upon reaching your next major pedestrian crossing to Faneuil Hall marketplace, now straight ahead in a redbrick complex built in 1742 next to an office tower. After exploring this dining and shopping mecca, cross North Street onto Union Street, continuing to follow the red line. You'll pass through a preserved district of old brick storefronts hosting many bustling restaurants.

You'll see many fountains shooting plumes of water vertically into the air during warmer months upon entering North End Park, which offers a refreshing respite from the city heat. Follow a brick sidewalk, and once through the park you'll be in the North End neighborhood, loaded with Italian eateries, many owned by the same family for generations, as well as markets on cobbled streets still lit with

Granary Burying Ground in the heart of downtown Boston

gas lamps. You'll see that this was Paul Revere's stomping grounds in a big way as you pass his house hidden behind a brick wall. Upon arriving at the Paul Revere Monument, look up and you'll see the Old North Church's white steeple. During the Revolution, Patriots signaled Charlestown that a British attack was about to take place. After passing the monument, you'll cross a brick-lined mall surrounded by an alley of trees past a fountain and up a set of stairs with the Copp's Hill Burying Ground to your right.

After crossing the Charlestown Bridge and turning onto Constitution Road with the river now to your right, you'll reach the USS *Constitution* aka *Old Ironsides*. This ship's thick oak bow earned its moniker by repelling a heavy barrage of mortar fire. After exploring the ship, museum, and visitor center, cross the street here on a wide green crosswalk, following signs pointing to the Bunker Hill Monument. Once you turn right, continuing to follow the red strip, you'll see the obelisk, similar to the Washington Monument, up ahead on Bunker Hill, commemorating a most pivotal battle in 1775. From here, retrace your steps back to the beginning of the route or take a bus or the T back to where you began.

MILES AND DIRECTIONS

0.0   Begin by paralleling Tremont Street to your right, walking on a sidewalk, and soon you'll see the visitor center off to your left.

0.3   After passing in front of the Massachusetts State House, turn right onto Park Street, heading back down the hill and paralleling the Common to your right.

0.5   Explore King's Chapel and an adjacent burial ground containing some ancient gravestones.

0.9   After exploring Faneuil Hall, cross North Street onto Union Street, continuing to follow the red line.

1.1   Cross diagonally to the left over to North End Park once you reach the intersection of Surface Road and Hanover Street.

1.3   Pass the Paul Revere House to your left behind a brick wall.

1.5   Reach the Paul Revere Monument.

2.6   Explore the USS *Constitution* and Visitors Center.

2.9   After taking time to explore the Bunker Hill Monument and Visitors Center, retrace your steps back to the nearest T or bus stop.

Inventing the Freedom Trail

It all began in 1951 with a man named Bill Schofield and an idea. As a veteran newspaper editor and daily columnist for the *Herald Traveler*, Schofield could find his way all over Boston nearly blindfolded, but when asked by tourists for directions to individual historic sites, he realized that even though they were within walking distance of each other, there was no organized route linking these gems together. He thought that if a native like him got lost, a tourist from Cincinnati was totally out of luck.

And so the Freedom Trail concept was born: connecting Boston's downtown and North End historic sites in an organized fashion with a walking route marked by attractive signs and arrows. Schofield fleshed out a trail prototype in his "Have You Heard" column and kept writing follow-up pieces on the idea. He pressed the fact that the project could be done on a budget of just a few dollars and a bucket of paint. His deliberate coverage paid off when he finally received a phone call from Mayor John B. Hynes pledging his support.

Throughout the years, the idea evolved from a purely City initiative to a coalition of public-private sector groups formed to open the first Freedom Trail information center on Boston Common, distributing free maps to a half-million visitors a year. By 1974, when the National Park Service stepped in, establishing the route as part of Boston National Historical Park, annual trail usage soared to four million.

Charles River Loop

Being a coastal city, you would think that the ocean would figure more prominently as a natural feature in Boston than a river could ever do. Then again, the Charles isn't just any river. Once a corridor for trade, it is now a recreational lifeline for Bostonians seeking respite from city life both on the water and, as you'll see throughout this route, land.

Start: After crossing the pedestrian footbridge from Embankment Road, turn left onto the pedestrian footpath

Nearest town: Boston

Distance: 7.6-mile loop

Approximate hiking time: 3 hours

Difficulty: Easy

Trail surface: Asphalt and concrete sidewalks

Seasons: Year-round

Other trail users: Rollerbladers, bikers

Canine compatibility: Dogs on leash permitted per city ordinances

Land status: Massachusetts Department of Recreation and Conservation

Fees and permits: None

Schedule: Sunrise to sunset daily

Maps: Rudimentary map available at www.mass.gov/dcr/parks /metroboston/maps/bikepaths _dudley.gif

Trail contacts: Department of Conservation and Recreation, 251 Causeway Street, Suite 600, Boston, MA 02114-2104; (617) 626-1250; mass.parks@state.ma.us

Finding the trailhead: Using the T, take the Green, Silver, or Orange lines to the Red line and get off at the Charles Street Station. Upon exiting the station, cross to Charles Street via crosswalk and then turn right, crossing Embankment Road to the pedestrian footbridge. GPS: N42 21.597 / W71 4.3759

THE HIKE

Minutes after progressing on the pedestrian footpath, you'll reach the Boston Community Boathouse alongside the paved pathway paralleling the Charles River close by to your right. After crossing a granite pedestrian bridge over a portion of the Charles River, you'll walk close by the river's edge, which is fairly level with the trail bed to your right. The waters of this river weren't always so approachable and were a virtual open sewer until the 1950s, when local conservation groups spurred a long and arduous cleanup. As late as the summer of 2007, the Charles River Swimming Club held their first 1-mile race in its waters. You'll pass an intersection where you'll see a bridge to your left crossing a portion of the Charles that's now closer by to your left. You can now clearly see that you are on a peninsula that's getting progressively narrower within the river.

Soon you will cross another pedestrian bridge over the inlet to several lagoons that you were just paralleling to your left. Now Storrow Drive will be immediately to your left through the park with the river continuing to your right. Upon reaching Harvard Bridge, climb the stairs up to the sidewalk above, turn right, and cross the river to Cambridge. Part of Harvard University's vast campus is plainly visible to your right along the riverbank. From here down to the Boston University Bridge, the trail is quiet and you're likely to see rowing teams skimming by, seemingly effortlessly plying the river's currents.

Downtown Boston skyline views from the shores of the Charles River

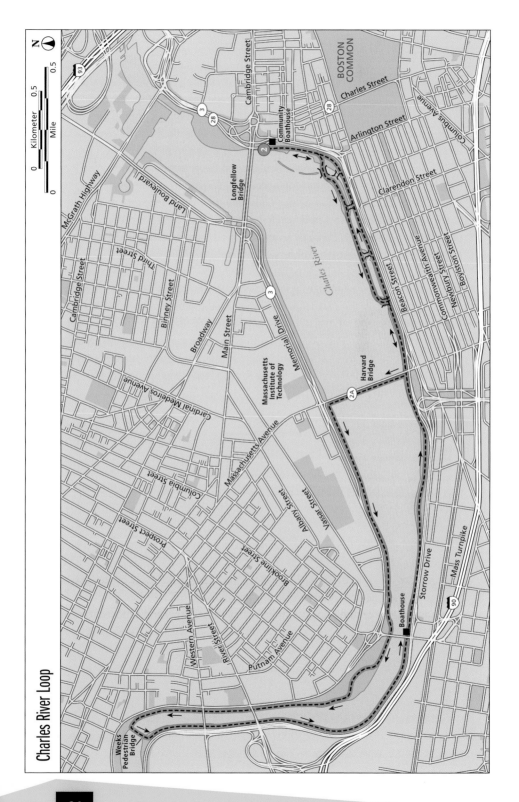

Charles River Loop

Bridge Fever on the Charles River

Many have heard of the gold rush out west or oil fever when black gold was first discovered in Texas. A lesser-known scramble for fortune began in 1786 on Boston's Charles River. John Hancock petitioned the General Court of Massachusetts for permission to build a toll bridge to link Charlestown with Boston. Hancock eventually got approval under the condition that he compensate Harvard College for fares lost to the school's existing ferry service. A second bridge, Francis Dana's Bridge, was built in 1793 using a more impressive design; more was charged for the privilege of crossing it. By 1808 an ostentatiously wealthy man named Andrew Craigie, who owned 300 acres in Cambridge and had the trustees of Harvard in his corner, built a third bridge against the wishes of both Dana and Hancock, who had by this time formed a partnership. By the time Isaac Livermore advanced his plans for a fourth bridge, the General Court had had enough. They granted rights but stipulated that upon reaching $150,000 in profits, Livermore was required to buy the Dana and Craigie bridges and turn them over along with his bridge to the Commonwealth. This action along with the coming railroad boom ended the easy money to be made on the Charles.

After passing the Boston University boathouse to your left, the trail closely parallels the river as you pass around the BU Bridge. Once you pass a soccer field and fitness station, bear left on a paved drive to reconnect with the riverbank, following it as it curves back to meet Memorial Drive. Soon you'll cross Cambridgeport and approach more of the Harvard campus. You'll cross two more bridges at River Street and Western Avenue, where at times you'll pass under sycamore trees planted in 1900 by landscape architect Charles Eliot.

Shortly after Western Avenue, where the river winds past a portion of Harvard's more ornate and majestic redbrick campus, continue following the walkway and turn left onto the John W. Weeks footbridge. Built in 1926 for students at Harvard Business School, it has the distinction of being the only footbridge across the Charles. Once on the opposite shore, the path is narrow and exposed to rushing traffic on Storrow Drive. You'll return to tranquility once you swing away from the riverbank at the BU Bridge. Here the boardwalk passes under a railroad trestle, reemerging at the BU Boathouse, where the path splits. Fork to the left, staying close to the river, and once you arrive back at the Harvard Bridge that you crossed earlier, continue straight and then bear left at the first footbridge to retrace your steps back to the chain of lagoons that you previously passed to your left.

Turn right at the next footbridge and reach a lagoon adorned with an Italianate fountain. After passing the second lagoon, you'll reach the Hatch Shell and then the Boston Community Boathouse docks. Continue retracing your steps back to the pedestrian bridge leading to the Charles Street T Station.

MILES AND DIRECTIONS

0.0 With the Longfellow Bridge to your right, turn left onto the pedestrian footpath.

0.1 Pass the Community Boathouse to your left.

0.3 Fork off to the right, crossing a granite pedestrian bridge.

0.7 Cross through an intersection, where you'll see a bridge to your left passing between lagoons.

0.9 Cross a pedestrian bridge over a long, narrow inlet that you were just paralleling to your left.

1.2 Turn right to cross the Harvard Bridge on Massachusetts Avenue to the north side of the river.

1.7 Turn left onto a walkway that parallels the river bank to your left. At this point walk along the river to the west southwest.

2.6 Continue on the river's edge after passing the Boston University Bridge on your left.

3.3 Pass the River Street Bridge on your left.

3.5 Pass the Western Avenue Bridge, still on your left.

3.8 Turn left, crossing over Weeks Pedestrian Bridge to the west or south bank of the river and turn to the south.

5.4 Pass the Boston University Boathouse on your left.

6.3 Pass the Harvard Bridge on your left.

7.5 Pass the Boston Community Boathouse, this time on your right.

7.6 Continue retracing your steps back to Longfellow Bridge and the pedestrian footbridge to your right.

Back Bay Fens: Isabella's Loop

What once was the mansion of Isabella Stewart, a wealthy Boston arts patron who at the turn of the twentieth century accumulated a massive collection of classical art from around the world, is now a museum dedicated to telling her life story. In addition to her lofty accomplishments, she was a loyal Boston Red Sox fan and loved horse racing. The grounds of this magnificent palace overlook the Back Bay Fens situated right across the Fenway. This route outlines where Isabella was known to frequently walk through this Olmsted-designed park.

Start: From the Isabella Stewart Gardner Museum, cross the Fenway to Back Bay Fens Park

Nearest town: Boston

Distance: 1.7-mile loop

Approximate hiking time: 1 hour

Difficulty: Easy

Trail surface: Clay, turf, pavement

Seasons: Year-round

Other trail users: Birders, joggers

Canine compatibility: Dogs on leash as per city ordinances

Land status: City of Boston

Fees and permits: None

Schedule: 7:30 a.m. to dusk daily

Maps: Rudimentary map available at www.cityofboston.gov/parks /pdfs/emeraldn.pdf

Trail contacts: City of Boston Parks and Recreation Department, 1010 Massachusetts Avenue, third floor, Boston, MA 02118; (617) 635-PARK (7275); Parks@cityof boston.gov

Finding the trailhead: *Inbound T Station:* Take the Green line to the Museum of Fine Arts T stop. Walk up Louis Prang Street, passing the Museum of Fine Arts to your right. Continue straight onto the Fenway for approximately 2 blocks, where you'll see the Isabella Stewart Gardner Museum to your left. The trailhead is to your right across the Fenway.
Outbound T Station: Take the Green line to the Longwood Medical Area T stop. Walk approximately ½ block up Longwood Avenue and turn right onto Palace Road. Walk up 3 blocks, first passing the Massachusetts College of Art campus and then the Isabella Stewart Gardner Museum to your right before reaching the Fenway. Cross here onto the pedestrian footpath trailhead. GPS: N42 20.3367 / W71 5.9418

From the Isabella Stewart Gardner Museum, cross the Fenway and proceed down an embankment onto a pedestrian pathway paralleling the Muddy River to your left. Soon you will bear right, sheltered by reeds and shrubbery passing a footbridge to your left. You'll see the stately granite Museum of Fine Arts and its School of Art come into view. After passing Forsythe Way to your right, which leads up to a small pocket park with the same name, you'll also see a gatehouse designed by H. H. Richardson. Just after passing underneath a large London plane tree, you'll reach Agassiz Road, named after geologist and glaciologist Louis Agassiz.

As you approach the Boston Conservatory, bear left at the fork to enter a playground called Mother's Rest that's artfully designed to escape the city bustle above. From here, climb steps decorated with an ornate handrail, returning to street level. After pausing to enjoy the views from H. H. Richardson's bridge, follow the path as it descends to the Fenway Victory Gardens. Established in 1942 in response to President Roosevelt's wartime initiative, this is the only World War II–vintage victory garden still in existence. Although not a part of Olmsted's design, there are 500 individual victory gardens in this vicinity covering seven acres that are worth checking out. Many are elaborate and have been tended by the same families for years. After exploring, continue on the paved path, and within a few steps, turn left at a trail intersection weaving through fruit trees.

Muddy river in Back Bay Fens

Back Bay Fens Rebirth

It's hard to imagine that simply walking along the shores of the Muddy River in the Back Bay Fens was at one time impossible. Throughout the Industrial Revolution, the Charles River and the Back Bay Fens were tied for holding the distinction of being the most polluted and fetid waters in all of Boston. Pressure was growing to contain an impending health crisis after years of serving as the city's open sewer and repository for anything unwanted, including hazardous manufacturing waste. The City of Boston responded in 1863 by passing the Parks Act and hiring the esteemed landscape architect Fredrick Law Olmsted. On the heels of completing New York City's Central Park, Olmsted now had an even greater challenge on his hands. Using tremendous engineering feats, Olmsted worked with city engineers to build sewers and redirect the freshwater Stony Brook River so the Fens could be entirely salt water. Next, two thirds of the Fens was dredged, filled, and graded. Every inch of this new parkland was then planted from scratch, using not only a huge amount of native species like beach plum and bayberry but also exotics like Oregon grapeholly, a native of the Pacific Northwest brought east by the Lewis and Clark expedition.

After paralleling Park Drive, you'll reach Agassiz Road, this time on the opposite bank of the Muddy River. From here, the trail curves to the left to a veteran's memorial and the Kelleher Rose Garden. This rose garden was designed by Olmsted protégé Arthur Shurcliff and opened in 1930. Continue through this meticulously maintained oasis of greenery showcasing more than 200 rose varieties to the arched exit. Continue by following the path leading to the playing fields and turn left once you reach a T intersection. Sweeping toward the Muddy River, you'll cross a pedestrian footbridge, completing the loop on this route. Turn right, retracing your steps back to the Isabella Stewart Gardner Museum.

MILES AND DIRECTIONS

0.0 Cross the Fenway from in front of the Isabella Stewart Gardner Museum.

0.3 Pass Forsythe Way to your right, which leads up to a small pocket park.

0.5 Cross Agassiz Road just after passing underneath a large London plane tree.

0.7 Enter Mother's Rest, a playground sheltered from the surrounding city noise.

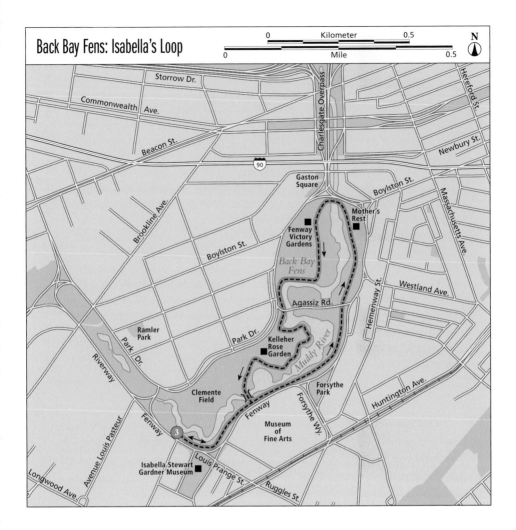

1.0 Descend on the footpath passing through the Fenway Victory Gardens.

1.3 Curve to the left, entering a veteran's memorial and the Kelleher Rose Garden.

1.5 Cross a pedestrian footbridge back over the Muddy River and turn right, now retracing your steps.

1.7 Return back to the Isabella Stewart Gardner Museum after crossing the Fenway.

Coastal Hikes

Shoreline at World's End Reservation (hike 8)

Shoreline view at Ellisville Harbor State Park (hike 9)

Prime birding and seal-watching venue.

Plum Island State Park: Sandy Point Loop

Walking along dunes and beach, you'll have scenic ocean and marsh views through-out most of this route. Perhaps the most remarkable feature is that after driving 6 miles down a dirt and gravel road along the length of Plum Island on the Atlantic Ocean, you'll soon see that not too far across the water, a heavy residential presence crowds the shoreline, serving as a strong reminder that the same fate would have befallen Sandy Point had it not been preserved.

Start: The trailhead begins on a wooden boardwalk to the left edge of a sand parking lot at the tip of Plum Island
Nearest town: Newburyport
Distance: 2-mile loop
Approximate hiking time: 1 hour
Difficulty: Easy
Trail surface: Sand
Seasons: Year-round
Other trail users: Birders, anglers
Canine compatibility: No dogs allowed

Land status: Massachusetts Department of Conservation and Recreation
Fees and permits: Entrance fee at gatehouse
Schedule: Sunrise to sunset daily
Maps: Visit www.topo.com
Trail contacts: Department of Conservation and Recreation, 251 Causeway Street, Suite 600, Boston, MA 02114-2104; (617) 626-1250

Finding the trailhead: From I-95, take exit 57, traveling east on Route 113. Continue straight onto Route 1A South for 3.5 miles and turn left onto Rolfe's Lane, following it 0.5 mile to its end. Turn right onto the Plum Island Turnpike and travel 2 miles, crossing the Sgt. Donald Wilkinson Bridge to Plum Island. Take your first right onto Sunset Drive and travel 0.5 mile to the Parker River Wildlife Refuge entrance. After paying your admission at the gatehouse, drive 6 miles down a sand and gravel road all the way to the end at Sandy Point. GPS: N42 42.1859 / W70 46.6822

THE HIKE

A s you approach Sandy Point at the end of Plum Island, you'll see a parking lot immediately to your left, but continue past this into another lot that this road dead-ends into. Begin hiking on a wooden boardwalk to your left, passing over dunes with a clear view of the ocean ahead. Once you reach the beach, turn right, walking down along the sand with the Atlantic surf to your left and dune grass close by to your right.

Rounding the point with an inlet and bay visible to your right, you'll pass mounds of driftwood, some pieces quite large, washed up into the dunes and on the beach closer along on this point as well. Once you're out on the sandy point, a roped-off area for nesting piping plover will be to your right for a stretch, and the sandy point resembles more of a large sandbar as you continue.

As you round the point, you'll be fully departing the ocean into the bay's protected leeward interior, sheltered from direct ocean breezes. Strictly dune grass yields to more of a wooded presence to your right along the shore with pine and underbrush. You'll be passing through portions of a tidal flat, but there is always enough beachhead through which to make a successful passage. Dune grass will soon once again be immediately to your right above the beachhead. The sand here is tightly packed rather than loose pebbled, making it ideal for

Dunes on Sandy Point

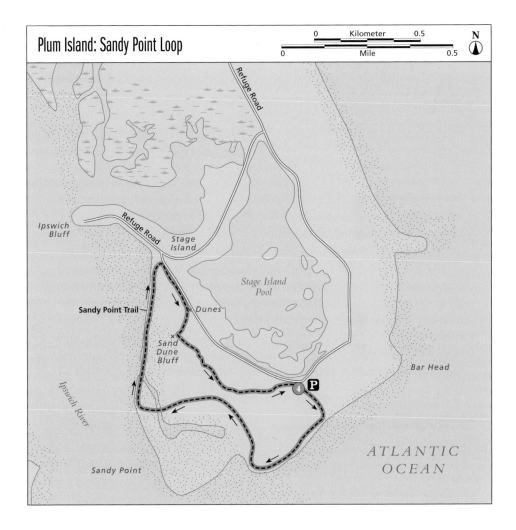

Refuge Road

Ipswich Bluff

Refuge Road

Stage Island

Stage Island Pool

Sandy Point Trail

Dunes

Sand Dune Bluff

Bar Head

Ipswich River

Sandy Point

ATLANTIC OCEAN

walking. The protected waters along this stretch host boat moorings and kayakers frequently paddling by.

Soon the water starts to get brackish close to shore since it's cut off by a sandbar. The beach also transitions to more of a mix of pebbles and shells instead of straight sand. The dune grass once more yields to thicker underbrush and trees. Turn right off the beach into the dune grass, where a brown sign with white lettering directs you onto Sandy Point. Here you'll also see another sign stating: Boundary Area beyond This Sign Closed to All Public Access.

As you continue on a lightly used footpath through the underbrush, you'll soon see a marsh off to your left; the trail surface can be wet at times depending on the season. The trail bed in this section of the route is not well established or demarcated. Once you reach a patch of sand that looks like a rough footpath to your right and can't continue straight any longer due to marsh, turn right, cutting into the dunes. Even though you won't see many footprints in the sand, you'll see rough outlines of trodden footpaths that have been used in the past. This condition is surprising for such a delicate ecosystem, but it's also a rare treat to be traversing this unique ecological wonder.

Treasure in Them There Sands

It's funny how the concept of treasure changes over time. Although most people would be thrilled to find a gold necklace encrusted with emeralds in the surf that washed up from a long-ago pirate wreck, perhaps the biggest treasure is to have wide-open, publicly accessible beaches from which to dream about such a scenario in the first place.

Sandy Point at the tip of Plum Island is one such spot that's steeped in lore and, as an added bonus, still remains just as wild and free as it was in 1635 when Reverend Thomas Parker arrived as one of the first Europeans on native soil. Later in 1907, island resident Albert Leet discovered a silver coin dated 1749. Soon after, another summer resident found Spanish silver buckles in the same location. You can be sure that yesterday, somebody was in the same spot with their metal detector, searching for what remains of this long-ago fortune.

The walking becomes more scenic when you cut to your left and climb up onto a sand dune bluff, which puts you up onto a ridge within the dunes. Most importantly, you'll catch ocean breezes once more, which are a welcome relief especially during the buggy spring and summer months.

You'll eventually curve to the left onto a more established footpath that's visibly trodden. You may see fresh deer tracks as this trail connects the shoreline now accessible down to your right with acres of dense thicket surrounding you. Soon you will return to the parking lot on the opposite end from where you began at the trailhead. Pass around a metal gate and return to your car.

0.0 Begin on a boardwalk over dunes with a clear view of the ocean ahead.

0.8 Round Sandy Point as the beach shoreline considerably narrows, and you'll be walking directly alongside the water's edge.

1.2 Pass shoreline that's noticeably more brackish close to shore since it's cut off by a sandbar.

1.3 Turn right off the beach into the dune grass, where a brown sign with white lettering directs you onto Sandy Point Trail.

1.4 Turn right, cutting into the dunes upon reaching a patch of sand to your right that looks like a rough footpath.

1.6 Cut to your left, climbing up onto a sand dune bluff.

1.8 Curve to the left onto a more established footpath through the sand.

2.0 Pass around a metal gate at the opposite end of the parking lot from where you began and return to your car.

Crane Beach: Dune Loop

Traverse wide-open sandy beaches alongside the surf to the deep sands of Crane Beach's highest inner dunes. If you can break away from your beach chair and the surf long enough to explore, you'll be rewarded with great coastal views and experience a microclimate within the dunes made possible by the bluffs' sheltering presence.

Start: From the out-of-town visitor parking lot to the right of the entrance, take the southernmost boardwalk to the beach

Nearest town: Ipswich

Distance: 5.9-mile loop

Approximate hiking time: 3 hours

Difficulty: Moderate

Trail surface: Sand with some rock

Seasons: Year-round

Other trail users: Birders, swimmers, anglers

Canine compatibility: Leashed dogs are permitted Oct 1 through Mar 31 but are restricted to below the high-tide line

Land status: Trustees of Reservations property

Fees and permits: Entrance fee

Schedule: 8:00 a.m. to sunset daily

Maps: Available at trailhead and www.thetrustees.org/assets /documents/places-to-visit/trail maps/Crane-Estate-Trail-Map.pdf

Trail contacts: Trustees of Reservations, (978) 526-8687; nergion@ttor.org; www .thetrustees.org

Finding the trailhead: From Route 128 north, take exit 20A to US 1A north and follow for 8 miles to Ipswich. Turn right onto Route 133 east and follow it for 1.5 miles. Turn left onto Northgate Road and proceed for 0.5 mile. Turn right onto Argilla Road and follow it for 2.5 miles to Crane Beach gatehouse at the end of the paved road. GPS: N42 41.0027 / W70 46.04

Crane Beach: Dune Loop

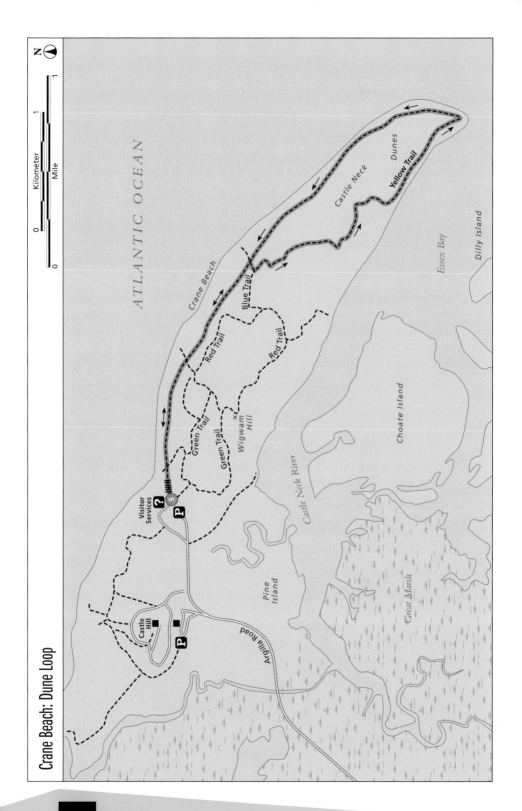

THE HIKE

From the out-of-town visitor parking lot to the right of the entrance, take the southernmost boardwalk to the beach. During summer, you'll certainly want to cast aside the shoes and sink your toes in the sand as you amble through the surf's foam. Depending on the tide level, you can either pass across loose, finely ground granite sand sparkling with mica or, in some patches, veins of feldspar that give the sand a purplish tint. The best part is that when you walk through these spots, the sand squeaks under your heels.

Looking ahead, you'll see Cape Ann against the horizon, and to your right, the dunes increase in elevation above the beachhead. Before turning right heading through a passage to the inner beach, wire fencing begins to restrict foot traffic to the seaweed-laced high-water mark. This marks off the nesting territory of the endangered piping plover. The wire now continues on either side of the sandy trail flanked by waves of dune grass. The trail grade gets steeper, cresting the dune several hundred feet in, and after walking down the other side, turn left, following the yellow markings.

From this point forward the dunes shield the trail surface from direct ocean breezes and biting salt air, creating a microclimate. You will likely see some different vegetation depending on the season, like mushrooms that when dry burst into

View of Crane Beach and dunes Photo courtesy of Amy Kvistad

star shapes dotting the trail in between the bayberry bushes. After winding along the rim of a bog to your right, the trail funnels through dune clefts before climbing to a sandy pinnacle overlooking the beach once again. From here you'll have clear views of Gloucester's Wingarsheek Beach on the opposite shore, the channel waters flowing past Conomo Point to Essex Harbor, and the uplands surrounding the Crane family's Great House.

Continue following numbered yellow trail markers leading across Castle Neck to a spot directly across from Hog Island. Although this island's name is pretty humdrum, few visitors realize that it served as the setting for Nicholas Hytner's film *Crucible*. During the summer months, this beach within a secluded cove has more visitors by boat than foot. You may also spot harbor seals sunning themselves on the rocks offshore. Depart the yellow trail and continue along a narrow beach, and as you round the peninsula's tip, the shore will broaden again once you're diagonally across from Gloucester's Halibut Point.

Soon as you bend to the left, Plum Island comes into view, followed by the cottages and the water tower on Great Neck, and finally Crane's Castle up on a hill. After walking the beach, the final long stretch of this route, cut back over the upland dunes, returning to the first of the two boardwalks. Turn left and retrace your steps back to the car.

Why Is It Called Crane Beach?

Chances are you've been in a public restroom and looked down at the toilet and saw Crane emblazoned on the bowl. Little did you know that this name is associated with Richard T. Crane, owner of Crane Plumbing, who in 1908 bought 250 acres of salt marsh, coastal drumlins, and wide-open meadows on the Atlantic Ocean for $125,000. And today, this is still some of the most spectacular beachfront on the eastern seaboard, all for the public to enjoy in perpetuity. But this reality wasn't always assured. Over the years, Crane expanded his holdings to 3,500 acres. In the 1920s nearby Ipswich residents were enraged that 5-mile Great Neck Beach had passed into Crane's hands without review, despite the town's claim of perpetual ownership. Crane responded by inviting Ipswich's entire school population to his son Cornelius's birthday party, which became an annual event. As time passed people grew accustomed to referring to the beach as Crane's. Then in 1945, fourteen years after her husband's death, Florence Crane made the ultimate charitable donation by giving most of Crane's Beach and Castle Neck to the Trustees of Reservations.

MILES AND DIRECTIONS

0.0 Take the long boardwalk at the head of the visitors' parking lot down to the beach.

1.4 Turn right through a passage to the inner beach with wire fencing on either side of the trail.

2.6 Depart the yellow trail, continuing along a thin fringe of beach as you round the peninsula's tip.

3.1 After crossing the first of two boardwalks, turn left and begin retracing your steps.

5.9 Arrive back at the trailhead.

🌿 Green Tip:
Before you start for home, ask yourself:
Have you left the wilderness as you'd want to see it?

6

Halibut Point Reservation

At first glance, Halibut Point appears to have always been an out-of-the-way nature preserve on a point jutting out into the Atlantic Ocean. Dig deeper into history, and you'll learn this secluded stretch of granite first started out as an outpost for a condemned woman during the Salem Witch Trials. A wilderness filled with bears, wolves, and Agawam natives, the area was not incorporated as an independent town until 1840, when granite quarrying was in full swing. Workers extracted large blocks of granite by hand, shipping them by sloop across the globe. Now the remaining open pits and piles of granite chunks stand as a reminder of this once-illustrious industry that ceased in 1929 with the Great Depression and the advent of concrete.

Start: Begin at the northwest corner of the parking lot off Gott Avenue
Nearest town: Rockport
Distance: 1.9-mile loop
Approximate hiking time: 1.5 hours
Difficulty: Moderate
Trail surface: Packed earth, sand, granite boulders
Seasons: Year-round
Other trail users: Birders
Canine compatibility: Dogs on leash allowed
Land status: Trustees of Reservations property

Fees and permits: Parking fee
Schedule: 8:00 a.m. to sunset daily
Maps: Available at visitor center, ranger's booth at the parking lot entrance, and www.thetrustees .org/assets/documents/places -to-visit/trailmaps/Halibut-Point -Reservation-Trail-Map.pdf
Trail contacts: Trustees of Reservations, (781) 784-0567; neregion@ttor.org; www .thetrustees.org

Finding the trailhead: Take Route 128 north of Boston toward Gloucester. At the first traffic circle, drive three-quarters of the way around, turning onto Route 127 toward Pigeon Cove. Continue 5 miles, and once you pass through the villages of Annesquam and Lanesville, the parking lot is 1 mile on Gott Avenue across from the Old Farm Inn. GPS: N42 41.2167 / W70 37.8607

THE HIKE

Cross Gott Avenue at the northwest corner of the parking lot to begin on a wooded footpath heading toward the visitor center. You will pass narrow trails to your right leading to two small quarries camouflaged by vines and underbrush. Upon reaching a wide-open T intersection, you'll feel the impact of ocean breezes and catch a view of the ocean in the distance. Directly in front of you, the enormous water-filled Babson Farm Quarry carved out in the mid-1800s lies below. By 1860, quarries on this reservation were at the height of their operation, employing more than 400 workers and supplying stone for Boston landmarks like the main post office and the Longfellow Bridge.

Fork to the right, continuing along the quarry's edge to your left on a gravel path through sparse sumac, cherry, and briars. You will pass markers along this stretch that provide a self-guided tour of quarry operations and how it impacted the landscape. At the next fork in the trail, turn right and you'll begin walking downhill away from the quarry on a narrow packed-earth path through rugged terrain. Once the trail levels out, turn left once you reach a four-way intersection and you'll be heading toward the ocean with the crashing surf now clearly audible.

Once you fork to the left with the ocean shore close by to your right, you'll pass through clusters of wild beach roses. During late spring and summer, the pinkish blossoms yield a sweet fragrance unlike any domesticated roses. Turn right at each

Babson Farm Quarry view Photo courtesy Mike O'Brien

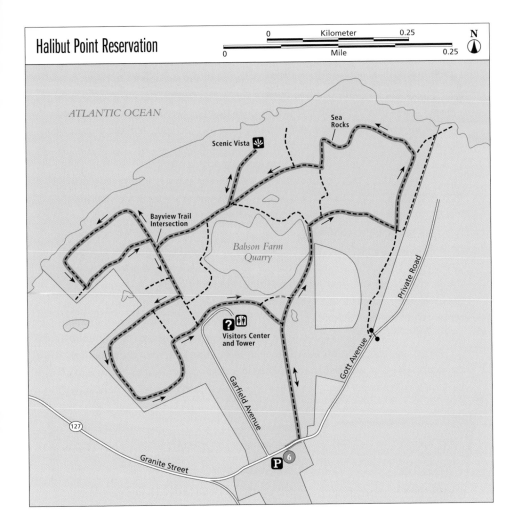

of the next three forks in the trail, veering ever closer to the sea, and soon you will reach a sign reading Sea Rocks This Way. These sea rocks are enormous boulders dotting Halibut Point's shoreline. Consisting of angular blocks mixed with irregular chunks tossed into heaps by thunderous surf and quarry workers long ago, they provide a dramatic setting for picnicking, surf casting, and rock hopping.

Continue with the crashing surf to your right, but be careful during low tide when kelp and sea moss cling to the rocks, making them treacherously slick. Up ahead you'll see a mountain of granite blocks tapering steeply to the sea. To experience its sheer size, walk or rock hop to the base of this boulder tumble. Backtrack from here and continue by turning right onto a broad sandy trail. The trail is not formally marked in this section, but you'll see a sign warning of the dangers of swimming off the point. Continue up a hill as the trail surface becomes gravelly, and you'll reach a peak amidst a pile of quarry debris. From here on a clear day, it's possible to see as far north as Maine's Mount Agamenticus and, in the nearer distance, Plum Island.

After continuing with more ocean views to your right, turn right and follow a wide path through birch, sumac, and cedar. A short way farther, turn onto the Bayview Trail, heading back toward the sea. This trail descends steeply then rises again as it curves to the left. Curving back uphill, the Bayview Trail loops past a grassy overlook. A small trail to your right leads to another lookout. Return to the Bayview Trail, following it to its end, and then continue ahead on a wide gravel path.

Once you reach a sign for the Back 40 Loop, turn left onto this grassy trail bed, walking downhill before swinging left once more on this serene lane. Once you reach the next intersection, continue straight, joining a trail that leads to the rear of the visitor center. Keep left to pass in front of the center, and from here the trail curves to the right, leading back to the wide-open intersection that you passed through at the beginning of your hike. Continue straight, retracing your steps back to the parking lot.

MILES AND DIRECTIONS

0.0   Cross Gott Avenue, beginning on a wooded trailhead.

0.1   Turn to the right upon reaching a broad T intersection.

0.2   Pass along the edge of Babson Farm Quarry to your left with interpretive signage.

0.6   Walk past sea rocks, enormous boulders dotting Halibut Point's shoreline.

0.8   Climb up on top of a pile of granite with spectacular horizon views.

1.0   Turn right at the Bayview Trail intersection.

1.7   Reach the visitor center, where facilities are available.

1.9   Reach the parking lot after turning right at the broad intersection and retracing your steps back to the parking area.

Coolidge Reservation

Get up close and personal with the North Shore's ocean front at this route's two farthest extremities. On one end you'll have an opportunity to stroll along a seawall and have a wide-open meadow, Ocean Lawn, to spread out your picnic lunch overlooking the ocean. This is where Thomas Jefferson's great-grandson built a grand cottage called Marble Palace. Walking to the other end, you'll have seasonal access along Gray Beach, an exclusive and extremely private beachfront enclave.

Start: Coolidge Reservation parking lot
Nearest town: Manchester-by-the-Sea
Distance: 1.5-miles out and back with a loop
Approximate hiking time: 1.5 hours
Difficulty: Easy
Trail surface: Packed earth and stone dust with some rock
Seasons: Year-round
Other trail users: Birders, anglers, and snowshoers

Canine compatibility: Dogs allowed
Land status: Trustees of Reservations property
Fees and permits: None
Schedule: Open dawn to dusk daily
Maps: On signboard and complimentary fold-up maps at trailhead
Trail contacts: Trustees of Reservations, (978) 526-8687; www.thetrustees.org; neregion@ttor.org

Finding the trailhead: Take exit 14 off Route 128 to Route 133. Follow Route 133 east for 3 miles and then turn right onto Route 127 South. Sign and parking area will be to your left in approximately 6 miles. GPS: N42 34.7911 / W70 43.5221

THE HIKE

You'll quickly ascend from the trailhead up the side of a ledge on a footpath curving through rugged, stony terrain surrounded by red pines sticking straight up all around. Keep climbing until you're standing up on a rock ridge overlooking the ocean on top of Bungalow Hill. After enjoying the view, continue following the trail, which passes the back side of this rock outcropping. Even though it isn't marked, you will see that the trail bed is worn into the forest floor as you're climbing down behind this rock ridge surrounded by mostly pine and a few scrubby oak. Once you intersect a level gravel path, you'll see Clarke Pond through underbrush straight ahead. Nearly a century ago, this pond was once a salt marsh until it was cut off from the tide when its inlet was filled, yielding a predominantly freshwater pond. Salt water still periodically washes in during high tides and storms, providing habitat for crabs and small saltwater fish.

Turn right and walk down this trail bed, which is fringed with a thin band of scrubby brush and oak on either side. The trail bed is slightly elevated here above the marshy pond to your left and extensive marsh continuing to your right. The vegetation surrounding the trail creates a tunnel effect due to how straight and continuous the trail extends into the distance. Soon you'll cross some large granite stones spanning an inflow/outflow stream connecting these two bodies of water.

View of Gray's Beach

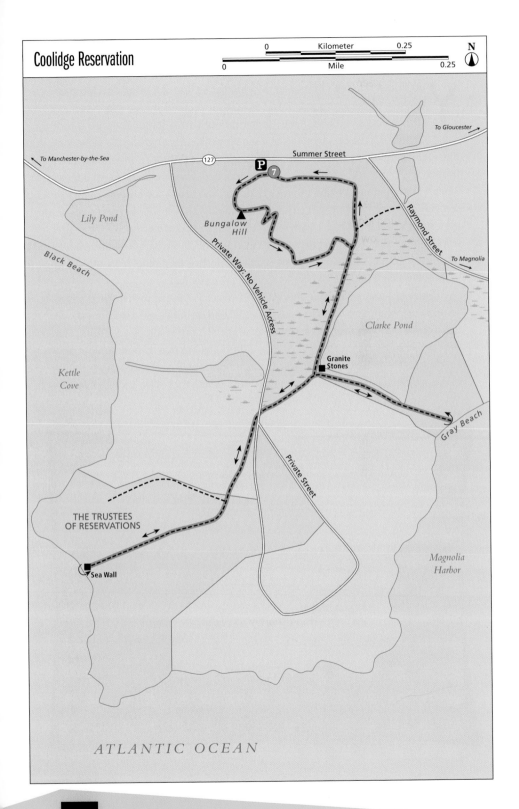

Coolidge Reservation

0   Kilometer   0.25

0   Mile   0.25

N

To Gloucester

To Manchester-by-the-Sea

Summer Street

127

P

7

Lily Pond

Bungalow Hill

Raymond Street

To Magnolia

Black Beach

Private Way: No Vehicle Access

Clarke Pond

Kettle Cove

Granite Stones

Gray Beach

Private Street

THE TRUSTEES OF RESERVATIONS

Sea Wall

Magnolia Harbor

ATLANTIC OCEAN

Within a few steps farther, you'll reach a split in the trail, where you want to turn right at a green sign with white lettering pointing to Ocean Lawn. The trail bed will continue on a level grade, but you'll pass through woods of mostly oak rather than marsh and underbrush. Cross a private paved road, and continue on the trail with a split rail fence flanking the right-hand side as you climb up a hill of cleared woods. Soon you'll cross another paved, private driveway; the split rail fence continues to the immediate right edge of the trail, and you'll emerge into a wide-open field with ocean views extending to the far edge of the field where it meets the shoreline. You'll soon be standing directly on slabs of blue slate outlining where the foundation of Thomas Jefferson's great-grandson's Marble Palace once stood. This meadow is inviting for enjoying a picnic lunch or strolling down along the waterfront on top of a seawall covered with concrete.

Ocean Lawn's Many Distinct Residences

It all began when Thomas Jefferson Coolidge purchased Millet's Neck for $12,000 in 1871 and renamed it Coolidge Point. He built the first residence, a large white clapboard summer cottage overlooking the deep blue Atlantic Ocean. This was razed in 1902, and in its place a Georgian mansion built mostly of brick with opulent trim was dubbed the "Marble Palace" after its marble foundation and extensive embellishments. Dignitaries such as President Woodrow Wilson and Norway's Crown Prince Olav were regular visitors until the 1940s, when it was razed to make room for another house in the 1950s, which was in turn leveled in 1989, leaving the Ocean Lawn as scenic open space.

Double back from Ocean Lawn, retracing your steps to the intersection near the granite blocks, but this time continue straight, following the sign pointing to Gray's Beach. The trail remains flat with a marsh visible through the brush to your left and a craggy rock ledge rising sharply to your right within the woods. After progressing a bit, you'll begin to hear waves crashing on the shore in the distance. Once you reach the beach, you'll see a sign indicating that this is Magnolia Beach, contradicting what the sign indicated earlier. The sign also reminds visitors that this beach is always closed to public swimming and closed to the public for strolling from May through September. So outside these months, you can stroll along the sand. From here, retrace your steps back to the three-way trail intersection, turn right, and head back to the parking lot.

0.0 Begin at the rear of a small parking area with a map board to your right off Route 127.

0.3 Turn right onto a level gravel path with Clarke Pond visible to your left.

0.4 Cross some large granite stones spanning an inflow/outflow stream connecting Clarke Pond to your left with marsh to your right.

0.5 Cross a private paved road and continue on a footpath with a split rail fence immediately to your right.

0.7 Emerge into Ocean Lawn with wide-open ocean views ahead at the far edge of the field as it meets the shore.

0.8 Stroll along the ocean front on top of a seawall.

1.0 Turn around to retrace your steps east, continuing straight through the T intersection and following the sign pointing to Gray Beach.

1.2 Turn around to rewalk the path past Clarke Pond and back to the T intersection. Turn right and retrace your steps back to the loop.

1.4 After passing a trail from the right, continue and turn left rather than continuing toward a gate fronting Route 127 visible in the distance.

1.5 Complete the loop back at the signboard and parking lot to your right.

🌿 Green Tip:
Printing out hike directions or a map at home uses less carbon than driving to a store to buy a map.

World's End Reservation

It's easy to see why this area has been dubbed World's End. Wide carriage roads wind high up through rolling meadows, providing ocean vistas and Boston skyline views. Fredrick Law Olmsted, designer of New York City's Central Park, was commissioned to design a housing development here in the late 1800s, but resident opposition stopped the construction. Next up, this bucolic peninsula overlooking Boston Harbor in the distance was on the short list for serving as the United Nations headquarters site, but New York City beat it out. Finally when a nuclear power plant was proposed here in the late 1970s, concerned citizens rallied together to preserve this tract of land once and for all. Enjoy their foresight on this route.

Start: Trailhead up an embankment from the first parking lot to your left

Nearest town: Hingham

Distance: 2.5-mile double loop

Approximate hiking time: 1.5 hours

Difficulty: Moderate

Trail surface: Packed earth, mowed grassland, and gravel

Seasons: Year-round

Other trail users: Birders, snowshoers, bikers, anglers

Canine compatibility: No dogs allowed

Land status: Trustees of Reservations property

Fees and permits: Fee for nonmembers

Schedule: 8:00 a.m. to sunset daily

Maps: Available at gatehouse and trailhead

Trail contacts: Trustees of Reservations, (978) 526-8687; neregion @ttor.org; www.thetrustees.org

Finding the trailhead: From Route 3, take exit 14 to Route 228 north. Travel approximately 6.5 miles and turn left onto Route 3A, traveling for approximately 1 mile. Turn right onto Summer Street, cross Rockland Street at the light, and follow Martin's Lane to the entrance and parking area. GPS: N42 34.7911 / W70 43.5221

THE HIKE

Begin at the first parking area to your left as you pass the gatehouse and pay your admission. Follow a gravel footpath leading up from the parking lot into cedar through a grassy picnic area. You'll see a tidal marsh in the distance to your right through the trees. Continue on this knoll, which has benches along the way for enjoying the sights.

Upon climbing down stone-block stairs, you'll now be on a stone dust–covered access road with split rails on either side. This road crosses a tidal inflow/outflow under the trail with close-up marsh views to your right and ocean waters lapping the shore to your left. After passing between these two bodies of water, you'll quickly approach a fork in the trail; you want to veer to the right, continuing on an access road fringing wide-open meadow to your left. The trail bed is level surrounded by midsize maple within rolling meadow and marsh views down below through underbrush. Here you'll see a windmill in the distance as well. You'll begin to hear surf crashing in the distance, and this sound will continue to be present on most of the route. You'll reach a good vantage point of a rocky cove surrounded by houses below through the meadow to your right, and the trail surface remains level with meadows rising up to your left.

You'll get your first blast of open ocean winds straight ahead and upon crossing a narrow isthmus connecting the two drumlins comprising this reservation. An

Carriage road leading through World's End Reservation

open-ocean bay to your left with a more protected cove to your right surrounds you for a short stretch. After being buffeted by ocean breezes, you'll emerge onto the access road, making a slight but steady climb up through rolling meadows once again, surrounded by clusters of large maple with water views continuing to your right.

Climbing at a slight grade, you'll reach a grand overlook with a bench. Here you can see an island straight ahead offshore with the Boston skyline in the distance and curving to the right above the treetops. The rocky cove that you encountered before is visible in the distance with houses clustered along the water's edge, giving it a San Francisco Bay appearance. Just a little past where you amble down away from this spot, ocean surf will be crashing down below through the trees to your right. After completing the loop within wide-open meadow, you'll head back between the two coves, but this time you'll climb another steady grade with open ocean views continuing to your right. As you're curving up into the meadow, you'll catch some more Boston skyline views over the water as well. Up to your left a rolling meadow extends upward on a hill, leaving you wondering what the views are like from atop this seemingly boundless meadow.

As you're curving away into the meadow's interior on a completely flat pitch, the ocean will no longer be close and visible to your right. Soon you'll be heading down a gradual pitch within the meadow with water views continuing through the trees, but after rounding a knoll, you'll notice that the ocean breezes dissipate dramatically. You'll complete the loop after heading down this gravel access road back at the map board. Retrace your steps from here by turning left and following the footpath back to the parking lot.

MILES AND DIRECTIONS

0.0   Begin at the first parking area to your left as you pass the gatehouse and pay your admission.

0.1   Turn right at a trail intersection with a map board immediately to your left. In about 300 feet, at a T intersection, turn right to start the first loop, heading north then northeast.

0.6   Reach a good vantage point of a rocky cove surrounded by houses below through the meadow to your right.

0.8   Reach a three-way intersection and experience your first blast of open ocean winds. Continue straight ahead (north) across the Bar connecting the two loops.

0.9   Pass a path coming in from the left; this is your return route. You're now on the north loop, which you'll walk counterclockwise.

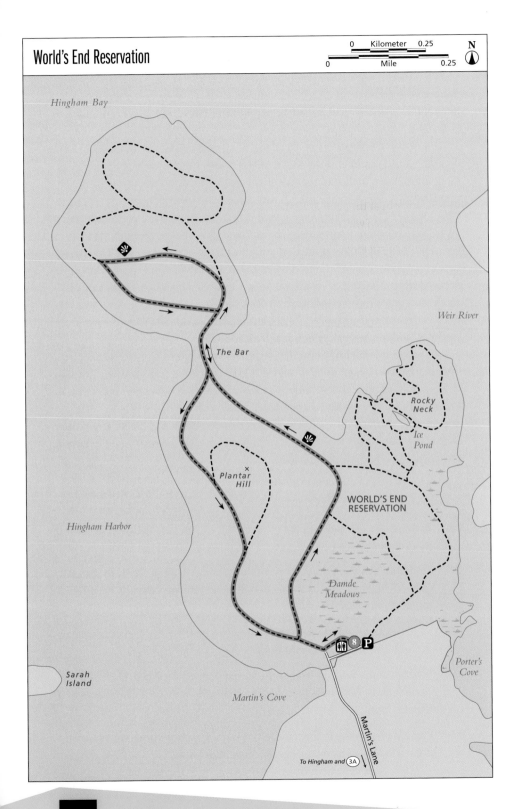

0   Kilometer   0.25

0   Mile   0.25

N

Hingham Bay

Weir River

The Bar

Rocky Neck

Ice Pond

×
Plantar Hill

Hingham Harbor

WORLD'S END RESERVATION

Damde Meadows

8   P

Sarah Island

Porter's Cove

Martin's Cove

Martin's Lane

To Hingham and 3A

1.0   Split to the left (northwest) and continue climbing at a slight grade.

1.3   Reach a grand overlook with Boston skyline views from a bench.

1.6   At a T intersection turn right to recross the Bar between the loops.

1.7   Veer right to walk the western half of the first loop southward.

1.9   Stay to the right as a path forks off to Brewer Grove. Climb up above the ocean moving into the interior of the meadow.

2.1   Keep right at the second Y intersection, after Planters Hill, heading down a gradual pitch within the meadow.

2.4   Continue straight or right at the third Y intersection.

2.5   Arrive back at the trailhead.

🌱 **Green Tip:**
*Never feed wild animals under any circumstances.
You may damage their health and
expose yourself (and them) to danger.*

Ellisville Harbor State Park

An ocean ramble at the southern end of Plymouth overlooking Cape Cod Bay, this park spans 101 acres of meadow, salt marsh, woodlands, and wide-open beachhead. One of the most scenic overlooks can actually be experienced from the parking lot. You'll see antique farm implements left over from a nineteenth-century farmstead that occupied the surrounding meadows and wide-open marsh and ocean in the background. This is prime birding and seal-watching habitat, so be sure to bring your binoculars.

Start: At the head of the parking lot to the left of a signboard on a level stone dust trail
Nearest town: Plymouth
Distance: 2 miles
Approximate hiking time: 1.5 hours
Difficulty: Easy
Trail surface: Stone dust and beach
Seasons: Year-round
Other trail users: Birders
Canine compatibility: Dogs on leash allowed

Land status: Massachusetts Department of Conservation and Recreation
Fees and permits: None
Schedule: Dawn to dusk daily
Maps: Available at www.topo.com
Trail contact: Massachusetts Department of Conservation and Recreation, Route 3A, Plymouth, MA 02362; (508) 866-2580; www .mass.gov/dcr

Finding the trailhead: Take Route 1A south about 12.5 miles from downtown Plymouth. Turn left onto a sand and gravel driveway at a brown sign with white lettering. The sign indicates that the park entrance is 1,000 feet ahead. Park in a large sand and gravel lot overlooking a saltwater marsh and the ocean down below. GPS: N42 34.7911 / W70 43.5221

A s you're walking across the parking lot, you'll get some good views of the marsh and ocean down to your right. Once on the stone dust trail bed, you'll be on a wide and level access road, and immediately down a bank to your right you'll be overlooking the marsh through gnarly oak and underbrush. To your left is an overgrown meadow that flanks the trail.

After continuing to your left at a fork on high flat ground progressing to an overlook with a picnic table to your right, you'll progress down a small hill surrounded by cedars with a band of meadow now on both sides of the trail. This is a good spot to look out for kestrels, which prefer to hunt in open meadows for small rodents and insects.

Water views continue through the trees to your right, and you'll cross a paved driveway passing a Conservation Commission building to your right. Continue straight, following a brown sign with white lettering and arrow pointing to the beach. You'll now be on a narrower stone dust path on a level grade up on a ridge closer to the ocean to your right. Before climbing down a set of wooden stairs directly to the beach, you can linger on a wooden viewing platform. Using your binoculars, scan the exposed rocks offshore at low tide for harbor seals. The best time to view these creatures is October through early spring, when they head down from Canada and Maine to warmer waters.

View of saltwater marsh from the parking lot

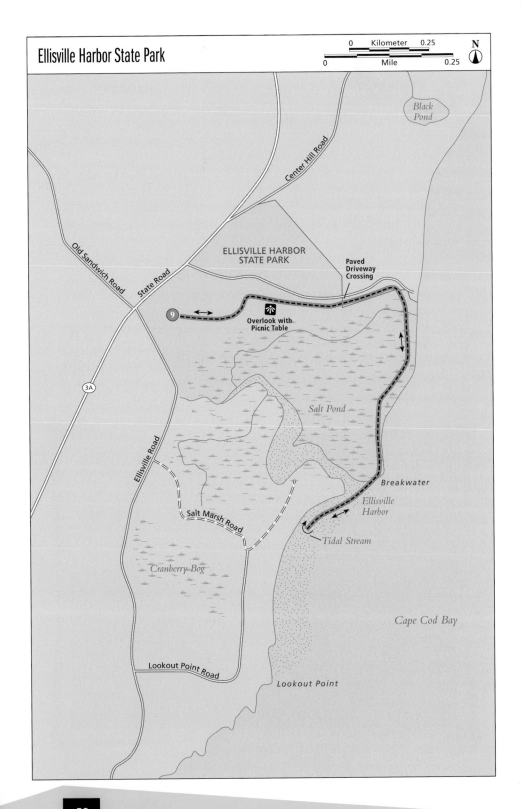

Ellisville Harbor State Park

0 Kilometer 0.25
0 Mile 0.25

N

Black
Pond

Center Hill Road

ELLISVILLE HARBOR
STATE PARK

Paved
Driveway
Crossing

Old Sandwich Road

State Road

9

Overlook with
Picnic Table

3A

Salt Pond

Ellisville Road

Breakwater

Ellisville
Harbor

Salt Marsh Road

Tidal Stream

Cranberry Bog

Cape Cod Bay

Lookout Point Road

Lookout Point

Once on the beach, turn right and walk over more stones than sand, particularly along the water's edge. Keep your eyes open for cormorants and buffleheads bobbing beyond the breakers and, during winter, the common loon with brownish gray feathers. Their quick flight movements are impressive for such a large bird.

Continue along this rugged coastline where the sand is concentrated to your right bordering the dune grass. Soon you'll have wider expanses of sand on the right with marsh in the distance and see steep sand cliffs sloping down toward the beach ahead in the distance. Once you reach a tidal stream, turn around and retrace your steps, unless you have the proper footwear to cross or it's warm enough to barefoot it.

MILES AND DIRECTIONS

0.0 Begin at the head of the parking lot with a brown signboard to your left.

0.1 Continue on high flat ground by forking to the left.

0.3 Pass an overlook with a picnic table to your right.

0.4 Cross a paved driveway, passing a Conservation Commission building to your right.

0.5 Enjoy a wooden viewing platform before walking down wooden steps directly onto the beach.

0.8 Cross a rough breakwater that ends at the surf line.

1.0 Turn around and retrace your steps upon reaching a tidal stream.

2.0 Return to the parking lot.

Overlooking the wide-open, blue Atlantic Ocean waters on Buzzards Bay, Horseneck Beach not only offers miles of expansive strolling and cool breezes but also plenty of opportunities for swimming and fishing. In addition, and near this route, Horseneck Beach State Reservation boasts 2 miles of wide, sandy shoreline more suitable for swimming.

Start: Begin walking down the stony shore of Westport Town Beach with Horseneck Beach Road directly to your right
Nearest town: Westport
Distance: 4.4-mile out-and-back
Approximate hiking time: 2 hours
Difficulty: Easy
Trail surface: Rocks, pavement, sand
Seasons: Year-round
Other trail users: Birders, saltwater anglers, swimmers

Canine compatibility: No dogs allowed
Land status: Department of Conservation and Recreation
Fees and permits: None
Schedule: Sunrise to sunset daily
Maps: At www.topo.com and by request at mass.parks@state.ma.us
Trail contacts: Department of Conservation and Recreation, 251 Causeway Street, Suite 600, Boston, MA 02114-2104; (617) 626-1250; mass.parks@state.ma.us

Finding the trailhead: Take I-93 south to Route 128 north, following it a short distance to Route 24 south. Follow Route 24 south to Fall River and the intersection with Route 195 East. Follow 195 east to exit 10 and Route 88 south. Continue south on Route 88 for 11 miles, following signs for Horseneck Beach. From the intersection of Horseneck Road and East Beach Road, begin walking along the stony shore of Westport Town Beach, paralleling the road to your right. GPS: N41 30.2513/W71 1.3642

THE HIKE

Posted signs indicate that you need a town permit to park on the side of East Beach Road that's directly on the shoreline. However, there aren't any signs across the street on the wide gravel shoulder indicating that it's prohibited to park here. Be aware that parking availability may also depend on the season and be harder to secure during the busy summer months. As you progress up the shoreline comprised entirely of mounds of granite rocks smoothed with continual wave action, you'll pass a line of mobile homes right on the water's edge. A little before the shoreline transitions from rock to a sandy surface, you'll make a quick right and then left onto East Beach Road, following it over a stone causeway built in 1924 and connecting Horseneck Beach with Gooseberry Island. Plenty of opportunities abound for ocean fishing on this stretch.

The pavement ends in a parking lot, and at the head of the parking lot to your right, you'll see the entrance to an access road behind a green metal gate. Pass around the gate onto a wide, sandy roadbed surrounded by beach plums; depending on the season, aromatic wild roses may be in bloom. Soon you'll curve into the interior of this island with the open ocean visible over low-lying vegetation on either side. You will pass access points to your right where you can easily reach the shoreline for a closer look.

Horseneck Beach

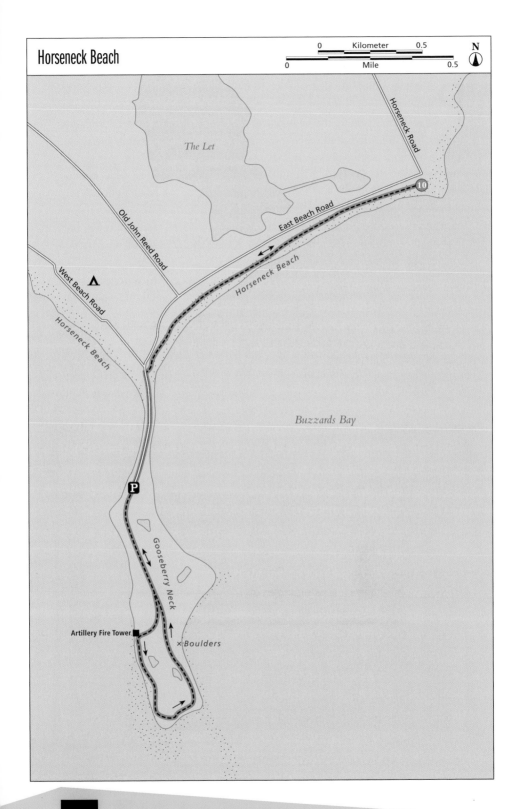

Horseneck Beach

The Let

Old John Reed Road

West Beach Road

Horseneck Beach

East Beach Road

Horseneck Road

10

Horseneck Beach

Buzzards Bay

P

Gooseberry Neck

Artillery Fire Tower

× Boulders

You'll be advancing toward a red-and-white tower off in the distance to your right, and as you progress notice traces of deteriorated asphalt indicating that this surface was once paved. After the hurricane of 1938 destroyed all the summer homes that were once on this peninsula, the U.S. Army constructed an artillery fire control base on the peninsula as part of a coastal defense system protecting the entrance to the Cape Cod Canal, 5 miles to the east. Remnants of this military occupation remain today, including portions of the observation towers and supply sheds.

The access road soon curves sharply to your right, and you'll be heading directly toward what you can now see is a graffiti-covered observation tower. After passing between this tower and an abandoned supply shed, the trail bed transitions to a footpath where you'll turn to the left, cutting through dune grass just before you reach the shoreline. The dune grass soon transitions to a more established footpath with a sandy surface paralleling a beach with open surf directly to your right. In the distance to your left will be a marsh.

Once you are walking on a sandy beach rather than a footpath, you'll soon pass a nesting area to your left fringed with wire. This protected area has you walking close alongside the water's edge as you're rounding a point where you'll begin to see the horizon of the mainland's far shore straight ahead in the distance. Once you round the point, you'll be within continuous sight of the mainland and see the military installations in the distance to your left. After traversing sand for a stretch, you'll now once again be passing over smooth granite rocks and then hit a sandy patch marked with several large boulders, providing a good resting

Beach art found on Horseneck Beach

place or picnic spot. After enjoying this area, retrace your steps a bit and look off to your right for footprints leading to a worn footpath that cuts up through dune grass and then dense briars and underbrush away from the ocean. Soon you will complete the loop within this route back onto the access road with the observation tower to your left. Continue straight, retracing your steps back to the parking area and causeway.

MILES AND DIRECTIONS

0.0 Begin walking along the stony shore of Westport Town Beach from the intersection of Horseneck Road and East Beach Road.

0.9 Cut to the right up off the beach and turn left, walking along East Beach Road.

1.1 Begin walking over a rocky causeway, continuing on a paved road with ocean on either side.

1.4 Enter a parking lot off this causeway onto Gooseberry Neck.

1.8 Curve sharply to the right at a three-way intersection, continuing on an access road heading directly toward a graffiti-covered artillery fire tower.

1.9 Turn left onto a footpath after continuing between the artillery fire tower and the supply shed.

2.0 Transition from a footpath to a wide sandy beachhead.

2.5 Enjoy a sandy patch with good horizon views of the mainland marked with some larger boulders.

4.4 Retrace your steps back over the causeway to where you parked alongside East Beach Road.

Inland Hikes

Trail bridge over Goat Hill Lock (hike 26)

Important regional ecosystem

Maudslay State Park

Right outside the seafaring town of Newburyport, Maudslay State Park encompasses a vast stretch of forest and rolling meadows high above the Merrimack River that has served as mansion grounds since the 1600s. First it was William Moulton who earned a fortune mining silver along the riverbanks, and then his descendant Henry built a gothic wooden castle on the highest point in 1860. In 1896 financier Charles Moseley tore it down, building his own seventy-two-room estate, and fashioned the grounds after Maudsleigh, his family's ancestral home in England.

Start: From the large dirt and gravel parking lot, cross Curzon Mill Road into a wide-open field lined with a stone wall and large oaks

Nearest town: Newburyport

Distance: 2.8-mile figure eight

Approximate hiking time: 1.5 hours

Difficulty: Moderate

Trail surface: Packed earth and gravel

Seasons: Year-round

Other trail users: Birders, snow-shoers, cross-country skiers

Canine compatibility: Dogs on leash allowed

Land status: Massachusetts Department of Conservation and Recreation

Fees and permits: Parking fee

Schedule: Dawn to dusk daily

Maps: Available at www.mass .gov/dcr/parks/trails/print /Maudslay.pdf

Trail contacts: Department of Conservation and Recreation, 251 Causeway Street, Suite 600, Boston, MA 02114-2104; (617) 626-1250; www.mass.gov/dcr/

Finding the trailhead: From north and south: Take exit 57 from I-95 to Route 113 east, following Route 113 for 0.5 mile. Turn left onto Noble Street, and at stop sign turn left onto Ferry Road. Bear left at the fork and follow signs. From west: Take exit 55 from I-495 to Route 110 East. Follow 1 mile to Merrill Street, turning right at the second light. Continue on Merrill Street/Spofford Street for 1.5 miles. Turn right before stop sign onto Ferry Road and follow the park signs. GPS: N42 49.2863/W70 55.5799

THE HIKE

C ross Curzon Mill Road from a large dirt and gravel parking lot into a wide-open field lined with a stone wall and large oaks. After passing a signboard to your left posted with notices, continue following a narrow footpath worn through the grass as it forks to the right and soon begins paralleling the tree line closer by to your left. You'll then depart the meadow into a forest of massive, widely spaced pine planted by Charles Moseley in the 1800s. The understory has been visibly cleared in between the trees so you can see for quite a distance across the forest floor. The trail surface is wide enough for a vehicle to pass through and heavily blanketed with wood chips so there is no doubt as to where to proceed.

Trail bed passing through pine forest

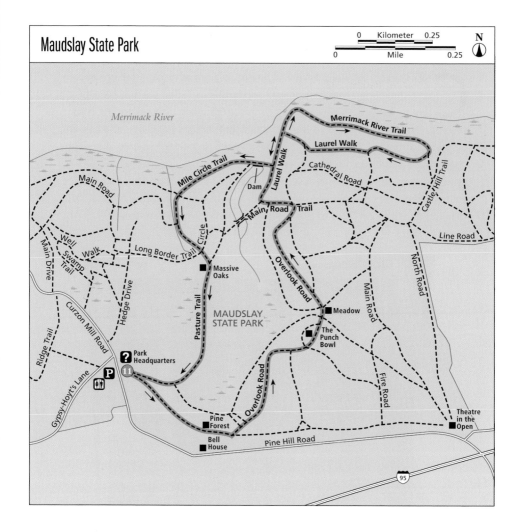

After departing these grand pines by turning left onto a narrower footpath heading down into thicker woods, you'll soon pass a meadow frequently filled with grazing deer bordering the woods line with a trail leading off to your right. Continue curving through the woods as it gets a bit thicker with maple on what is now a level carriage road. Dense tree cover hides a steep and long embankment down to your right, and you'll faintly see a meadow in the distance through the trees.

Once you turn left into a meadow at a three-way intersection, the trail bed transitions to gravel, and as you progress through the meadow, you'll see a stone bridge straight ahead. At your next intersection, veer to the right on an access road away from the bridge, out of the meadow, and you'll start to get your first glimpses of the Merrimack River ahead down through the forest. Soon you'll pass a brook to your left, which leads to a stone spillway that you'll also pass to your left. After continuing straight, the trail curves to the right, paralleling the river from high up above the water. Periodic side trails lead to the cliff's edge for better water views.

You'll see a marina across the river on the opposite bank, and thick rhododendrons cluster along the right edge. If you're visiting in early June, you'll experience a proliferation of aromatic white blossoms. Down below on the water during the warmer months, you'll notice a high level of boating activity, and on the opposite shore will be a heavy residential presence, a sharp contrast from the seclusion that engulfs you on the trail.

After looping up into the woods away from the river, through thick rhododendron groves, retracing your steps back to the stone spillway now to your right, cross over the top. After doing so, you'll curve to the left alongside what remains of a small mill pond above the dam. Above the pond, you'll be on a wider access road curving up onto a ridge, once more overlooking the river. This time you're higher up and the roadbed is much wider, clear, and well established. Upon passing through wide-open pine, you'll begin cutting to the left away from river views, eventually passing a stone bridge to your right leading up into the woods.

Once you are passing through some massive oaks within a clearing, you'll begin to see that you're heading back up toward a meadow in the distance. Once you emerge into this meadow, you'll be on a sand and gravel access road with the woods line in the distance to your right. Depending on the season, chances are good that numerous wildflowers like black-eyed Susan and Queen Anne's lace

Millpond spillway

will be blossoming throughout the meadow grass. You'll soon see the parking lot ahead in the distance across Curzon Mill Road, indicating that you're completing the loop. Just before reaching the road that's visible straight ahead, turn left onto a worn footpath through the grass, completing the route back at the signboard. Retrace your steps, passing back through the stone wall to the parking lot.

MILES AND DIRECTIONS

0.0 Cross Curzon Mill Road, passing through a stone wall, where you'll see a signboard to your left posted with notices. Proceed to the right of this sign into the field.

0.3 Depart the meadow, passing into a wide-open expanse of pine forest.

0.4 Turn left at a T intersection, departing these grand pines onto a narrower footpath (Overlook Road).

0.5 Turn right and head through deep forest at a T intersection.

0.7 Pass a meadow bordering the woods line with a trail leading off to your right.

1.0 Turn left into a meadow at a three-way intersection onto the Main Road Trail where the trail surface transitions to gravel.

1.5 Curve to the right at a fork in the trail onto Laurel Walk, soon passing through large pine and thick rhododendron.

1.7 Pass straight through another intersection onto the Merrimack River Trail, and you'll see the river though the trees.

2.0 Turn right at a T intersection onto a wider access road curving up onto a ridge.

2.2 Turn right at another T intersection onto Mile Circle Trail passing a stone bridge to your right leading up into the woods.

2.3 Turn right, heading through some massive oaks within a clearing as you're heading up toward a meadow in the distance.

2.8 Passing back through the stone wall and completing the second loop, retrace your steps back to the parking lot.

Weir Hill Reservation

Once part of a 500-acre estate built by nineteenth-century industrialist Moses Stevens, this route encompasses a distinct mix of wide-open meadow views of Lake Cochichewick and dense forest bordering the water's edge. This reservation was named after the fish weirs (woven fences) that natives used in nearby Cochichewick Brook to trap fish swimming toward the lake.

Start: Map board alongside Stevens Street
Nearest town: North Andover
Distance: 2.2-mile loop
Approximate hiking time: 1.5 hours
Difficulty: Moderate
Trail surface: Packed earth, gravel, and rock
Seasons: Year-round
Other trail users: Birders and snowshoers
Canine compatibility: Dogs on leash permitted

Land status: Trustees of Reservations Property
Fees and permits: None
Schedule: Open 8:00 a.m. to sunset daily
Maps: On signboard at trailhead and available for purchase at gift shop
Trail contacts: Trustees of Reservations, (978) 682-3580; www.thetrustees.org; neregion @ttor.org

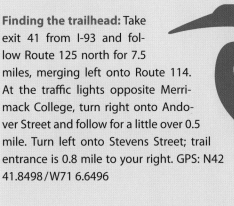

Finding the trailhead: Take exit 41 from I-93 and follow Route 125 north for 7.5 miles, merging left onto Route 114. At the traffic lights opposite Merrimack College, turn right onto Andover Street and follow for a little over 0.5 mile. Turn left onto Stevens Street; trail entrance is 0.8 mile to your right. GPS: N42 41.8498 / W71 6.6496

Begin at a map board, which contains giveaway pocket maps, to the left of the trailhead. Pass through an overgrown meadow underneath some large maples. As soon as you cross through the stone wall at the back edge of this meadow, turn right at a three-way trail intersection onto the Stevens Trail, beginning a long, steady climb on a wide trail surface maintained with erosion bars at different intervals and surrounded by medium-growth oak, ash, and maple. The trail levels out as you emerge into a field high up on a ridge where you'll have some wide-open views of the Merrimack Valley down below in the distance to your right. A bench has been installed here as well to encourage hikers to relax and linger.

After rounding the crest of this field, you'll begin making a steady descent through this field, which narrows on either side and is interspersed with oak. You'll get your first wooded views of Stevens Pond, a much smaller body of water connected to Lake Cochichewick, down to your right. The trail levels off soon as you're closer and more level with the lakeshore to your right. You'll depart from the meadow into the woods on a level wood road with the pond even more visible through the trees to your right. Here you'll be walking along a ridge within the woods, and soon you'll also see Lake Cochichewick ahead through the trees.

After passing a trail spur to your right leading down to a town beach (open to North Andover residents only) on Stevens Pond, you'll be skirting the shores of

View of Lake Chochichewick from trail

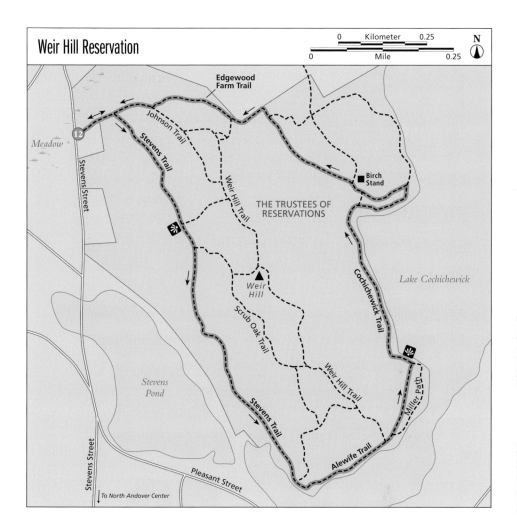

Lake Cochichewick, a large body reservoir close by to your right. Medium oak and small pine on a steep embankment separate you from the water's edge. The trail bed remains level, passing through what appears to have been at one time open meadow. You'll now have a sense that the lake is long and narrow through the wide-open forest canopy populated with large oak. Continue along the trail bed, cutting into what at times will be a steep embankment down to the water's edge

🍂 **Green Tip:**
For rest stops, go off-trail so others won't have to get around you. Head for resilient surfaces without vegetation.

after reaching a clear overlook of the lake. If you look closely, you'll see pieces of a broken chimney to your right on this wooded peninsula. It is here that nineteenth-century industrialist Moses Stevens helped found the North Andover Country Club, which is now located across the lake.

Be sure to turn left sharply up and away from the lakeshore, following a wood road up into the forest. You'll pass through a pine grove and pass a condominium complex close through the trees to your right before completing the loop back at the overgrown meadow surrounded by maples.

MILES AND DIRECTIONS

0.0   Begin at trailhead to the right of a map board with giveaway trail maps.

0.1   Cross through a stone wall at the back edge of the field and turn right onto the Stevens Trail.

0.3   Emerge into a meadow where the trail levels out high up on a ridge.

0.4   Enjoy your first wooded views of Stevens Pond down to your right.

0.6   Depart from the meadow into the woods on a level wood road.

0.8   Continue straight through an intersection where a trail spur to your right leads down to a town beach on Stevens Pond.

1.0   Begin skirting the shores of Lake Cochichewick close by to your right.

1.2   Enjoy clear views of the lake.

1.5   Turn sharply left on a wooded but cleared peninsula away from the lakeshore, following a wood road up into the woods.

2.2   Complete loop back through field to the map board alongside Stevens Street.

Skug River Loop

This hike will take you over and around the Skug River , which is named after a phonetic spelling of the Nipmuc word for "skunk." Passing over and close by long stretches of marsh, this loop is most obviously a destination for wildlife viewing. Less readily apparent surprises you'll encounter along the way are remnants of a gristmill, a soapstone quarry, farms, and a large glacial erratic sticking out of the forest floor.

Start: Begin off Korinthian Way at a brown sign with yellow lettering indicating that this is the Mary French Reservation
Nearest town: Andover
Distance: 2.4-mile loop
Approximate hiking time: 1.5 hours
Difficulty: Easy
Trail surface: Packed earth and boardwalks
Seasons: Year-round
Other trail users: Birders

Canine compatibility: No dogs allowed
Land status: Andover Village Improvement Society
Fees and permits: None
Schedule: Sunrise to sunset daily
Maps: Rough maps available at www.avisandover.org/maps /SkugHammond.pdf
Trail contacts: AVIS, P.O. Box 5097, Andover, MA 01810; (978) 475-3595; info@avisandover.org

Finding the trailhead: Off I-93, take exit 41, bearing right onto Route 125. After 4.5 miles, turn right onto Salem Street and continue straight onto Gray Road. After just under 0.5 mile, turn right onto Korinthian Way and park at the dip just before Athena Circle. GPS: N42 37.7964/W71 6.0498

THE HIKE

The trailhead is easy to miss but is visibly well marked once you spot it off Korinthian Way in a residential neighborhood. In the patch of woods alongside the street, you'll see a brown sign with yellow lettering indicating that this is the Mary French Reservation. Farther in to your right along the trail, you'll see another sign indicating that this is Andover Conservation Area land. You will also see two white markings pointing to the right as well as a sign marker indicating that you are also on the Bay Circuit Trail.

More about the Bay Circuit Trail

Out of all the routes covered in this book, the Skug River Loop follows the longest stretch of the Bay Circuit Trail. The signs are frequent, highly visible, and may just inspire you to continue following the Bay Circuit through its entire length. A permanent recreation trail and greenway corridor linking parks and open spaces surrounding the entire metropolitan Boston, it was first proposed in 1929 as an outer emerald necklace. The trail currently starts on the North Shore's Plum Island, linking parks, open spaces, and waterways all the way to Kingston Bay on the South Shore. Gaps remain, but gradually the missing links on this 200-mile corridor of fifty cities and towns are being connected to ultimately span more than eighty-five areas of protected land. Several groups and individuals have already traversed the entire 200-mile trail with the necessary detours.

Passing rocks below the roadbed, you'll be walking in on a stone dust trail bed past backyards of the surrounding residences through the trees on either side as you progress. You'll soon traverse a boardwalk over wooded marsh and then onto wooden planks, where you'll be up close and personal above a full marsh replete with thick cattails on either side. This provides a perfect vantage point for viewing wood ducks and cranes.

Upon departing the boardwalk, you'll soon turn right onto an earthen causeway elevating the trail bed above the marsh. This was built by farmers at the turn of the century to create a watering hole for cattle and an ice pond. Once you depart the marsh, you'll be traveling through many small pine and larger oak.

After crossing Salem Street, enter a dirt parking lot with a display board of trail photos and a sign indicating that this is the Skug River Reservation. Pass to the left of the display board, following the white blazes onto a footpath, and within steps you'll be on a well-constructed boardwalk traversing marsh once again. Winding over wooded marsh, you'll still have a residential presence through the trees to your right. Once you reach a small sign up on a tree reading Bridge Trail, you'll turn right onto another boardwalk, this time crossing a slow-moving creek. As soon as you pass over the boardwalk, you'll see small blue triangles on the trees as you wind up away from wooded marsh into thicker pine and oak. The trail bed is wide and carpeted with pine needles.

As you begin down a hill with a marsh to your right reaching close up to the trail bed, you'll follow a faint white arrow up on a tree pointing to your left. Once you begin hearing a stream and see it down to your left, you'll reach gristmill ruins to your left, and behind this is a marsh that the Skug River is emptying from as it flows toward you. Here is a good viewing area for blue heron if you're extra quiet.

Continue paralleling the Skug River close by to your left, which is really a swift-flowing stream. As soon as you see a wooden footbridge to your left, cross over the river, and soon wide-open marsh will be close by to your right through a thin band of trees. Some old stone foundations, which are the remains of a soapstone quarry, are immediately to your left as you continue on a ridge overlooking the marsh.

Boardwalk over Mary French Reservation marsh

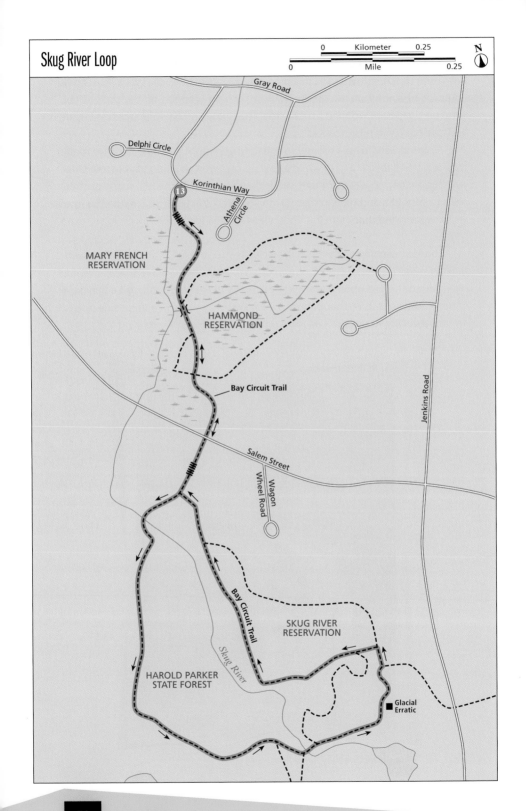

Skug River Loop

0 Kilometer 0.25
0 Mile 0.25

N

Gray Road

Delphi Circle

Korinthian Way

13

Athena Circle

MARY FRENCH RESERVATION

HAMMOND RESERVATION

Bay Circuit Trail

Jenkins Road

Salem Street

Wagon Wheel Road

Bay Circuit Trail

SKUG RIVER RESERVATION

Skug River

HAROLD PARKER STATE FOREST

Glacial Erratic

You'll soon pass a glacial erratic, a huge upended boulder the size of a pickup truck. The forest floor in this vicinity is remarkably wide open to your left with almost all medium-size oak scattered across the rocky forest floor.

Once you climb over a small planked footbridge, you'll see a small brown sign with yellow lettering indicating that you're heading back into the Skug River Reservation. Continue through widely spaced oaks following the white blazes, and you'll see another sign marking this as part of the Bay Circuit Trail. Gradually the trail bed climbs up onto a slightly higher elevation from the rest of the forest floor. After turning right back through a stone wall marked with white squares on the trees, retrace your steps back to where you started.

MILES AND DIRECTIONS

0.0 Begin off Korinthian Way in a residential neighborhood where you'll see signs indicating that this is the Mary French Reservation and Andover Conservation Area land.

0.2 Turn right onto an elevated trail bed built up with rock into a type of dike above the marsh marked with white blazes on the trees.

0.4 Cross Salem Street, entering a dirt parking lot with photos of the trail ahead affixed to a display board.

0.5 Turn right onto a boardwalk once you reach a small sign up on a tree reading Bridge Trail.

0.9 Turn left at a T intersection with a vast marsh visible straight ahead through the trees.

1.0 Turn left at a three-way intersection marked with a faint white arrow up on a tree pointing in this direction.

1.2 Continue to the left at a fork in the trail, where you'll hear a stream before seeing it down to your left.

1.4 Pass a huge glacial erratic, a boulder poking up straight from the ground seemingly from out of nowhere.

1.5 Turn left over a small planked footbridge, and straight ahead you'll see a small brown sign with yellow lettering indicating that you're heading back into the Skug River Reservation.

1.8 Continue straight at a fork in the trail, and soon you'll see another Bay Circuit Trail sign.

2.4 Arrive back at the trailhead.

Ward Reservation

Beginning through rolling meadows and farmland, you'll quickly climb up to Holt Hill, where you'll be treated to expansive views of the Boston skyline on the horizon as you stand amidst a ring of solstice stones. Soon you will be hiking deep into the forest fringing a large marsh with some spectacular birding opportunities.

Start: Parking lot off Prospect Road

Nearest town: Andover

Distance: 3.1-mile double loop

Approximate hiking time: 2 hours

Difficulty: Easy

Trail surface: Gravel, paved, earth, rock

Seasons: Year-round

Other trail users: Birders, snowshoers

Canine compatibility: Dogs permitted

Land status: Trustees of Reservations property

Fees and permits: None

Schedule: Dawn to dusk daily

Maps: On signboard and complimentary fold-up maps at trailhead

Trail contacts: Trustees of Reservations, (978) 682-3580; www.thetrustees.org; neregion @ttor.org

Finding the trailhead: Take Route 114 east from I-495 for about 2 miles and then turn right onto Route 125 South. After approximately 1.5 miles, turn left onto Prospect Road and look out for the parking lot to your right. GPS: N42 38.416 / W71 6.7456

THE HIKE

After walking briefly (about 200 feet) along Prospect Road through a residential area, you'll begin climbing a hill toward a stand of large pines up ahead to your left. You'll quickly turn right at a green metal gate up through the pines onto a footpath toward Holt Hill, the highest point in Essex County, and the solstice stones. This path soon opens up onto a grass-covered wagon road within a hilly apple orchard mostly to your left up on a ridge. You'll pass under some tall red pines as the wagon road now straddles two fields, and to your right down in a meadow, you'll see a working farm and in the distance out on the horizon, you'll have good views of the Boston skyline.

Follow white square blazes through a confusing trail intersection onto a well-established wood road that forks off into thick red pine high up on a ridge. You're steadily gaining in elevation under cover of thick pine until you emerge into another field, where the wagon road continues with a gradual climb up through meadow grass with the woods line close to your left. Radio towers on Holt Hill emerge into view up ahead to your left. Once on top of this 420-foot hill, you'll have a wide-open overlook through the meadow, giving you faraway yet clear views of the Boston skyline. In June of 1775, residents of Andover and North Andover climbed to the top of this hill and watched the burning of Charlestown during the Revolutionary War.

Working farm adjacent to the reservation

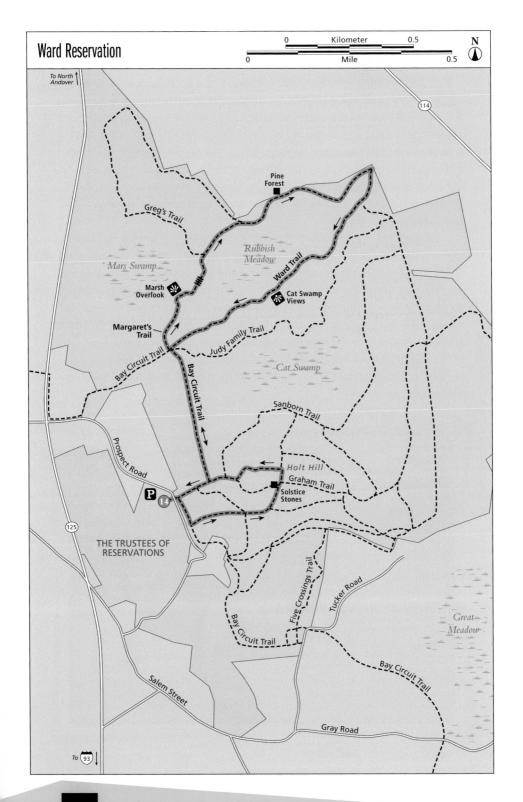

Ward Reservation

To North Andover

Greg's Trail

Pine Forest

Rubbish Meadow

Mars Swamp

Marsh Overlook

Ward Trail

Cat Swamp Views

Margaret's Trail

Bay Circuit Trail

Judy Family Trail

Cat Swamp

Bay Circuit Trail

Sanborn Trail

Prospect Road

Holt Hill

Graham Trail

Solstice Stones

P 14

THE TRUSTEES OF RESERVATIONS

Five Crossings Trail

Tucker Road

Great Meadow

Bay Circuit Trail

Salem Street

Bay Circuit Trail

Gray Road

To 93

N

0   Kilometer   0.5
0   Mile   0.5

Stonehenge of Andover

Mabel Ward donated the original land for the reservation in honor of her husband, Charles, who died in 1933. Then, inspired by an earlier visit to Stonehenge in England, Mabel had the solstice stones placed at the top of the hill in 1940. The circular arrangement uses the sun to tell time based on the resulting shadows.

After enjoying this dramatic resting place, perfect for spreading out a picnic lunch, continue on the meadow lane up behind the solstice stones toward the radio tower, which soon transitions to a paved access road. Follow the road downhill as it winds around a large concrete water holding tank immediately to your left. Once you turn right back into the woods, you'll now be on the Bay Circuit Trail, a regional greenway encircling Boston and linking the North Shore with the South Shore.

Passing through an intersection with Ward Trail and onto Margaret's Trail, you'll now pass over more rugged terrain on a rock ledge surrounded by a mix of thick pine and some oak. You'll soon see an extensive marsh down through the trees to your left as you pass on top of a prominent rock ridge punctuated with a large round boulder. You'll begin to pass over a wooden boardwalk fringing the marsh with a dam and small spillway to your right. A few steps after crossing this boardwalk, you'll cross another small wooden footbridge over a stream emptying from the marsh. Keep your eye out for kingfishers and mallards. After moving away from the marsh's edge, you'll cross a wooden footbridge over a stream; notice that you're passing between marshes on either side of the trail through the trees.

On your circuit back on the Ward Trail, you'll have a respectable vantage point of Cat Swamp down below the trees to your left. It is here that you're in the farther reaches of this 700-acre preserve, and chances are good that you'll have the trail to yourself. Complete the loop back at the intersection with the Bay Circuit Trail and retrace your steps back to the parking lot.

MILES AND DIRECTIONS

0.0 Double back and turn right onto Prospect Road from the parking lot.

0.1 Turn left off Prospect Road at a green metal gate fronting an access road, then quickly turn right at this gate up through the pines onto a footpath.

0.3 Turn left onto a well-established wood road into thick red pine.

14

0.5   Emerge from stately pine into another field.

0.6   Reach the top of Holt Hill surrounded by solstice stones with radio towers in the background and a wide-open meadow ahead with faraway yet clear views of the Boston skyline.

0.7   Turn right off access road onto a white-blazed footpath, Bay Circuit Trail.

1.0   Pass over a seasonal stream on a narrow, wooden plank walkway.

1.1   Fork to the left then take a quick right onto Margaret's Trail at the intersection (Ward Trail is the other leg) flanked by a stone wall.

1.2   Traverse a prominent rock ridge marked with a boulder overlooking the marsh.

1.3   Pass over a wooden boardwalk fringing the marsh to your left.

1.5   Continue straight at a trail intersection after moving away from the marsh's edge into rugged forest.

1.6   Pass a thick pine forest immediately to your left behind a stone wall.

1.9   Turn sharply right at a T intersection onto the Ward Trail.

2.3   View Cat Swamp through the trees to your left.

2.5   Return to the intersection with Margaret's Trail and Bay Circuit Trail, completing the northern loop. Turn left onto Bay Circuit Trail, heading south.

2.9   Return to the T with the access road, the southern loop, and turn right.

3.0   Pass straight through the gate and turn right onto Prospect.

3.1   Retracing your steps on Prospect Road, return to the parking lot.

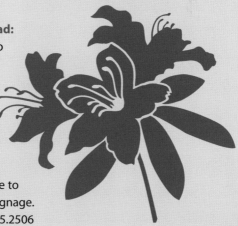

Ipswich River Wildlife Sanctuary

Ensconced within the protected lands of the Ipswich Audubon Society, many landscape variations intrigue the senses. This route covers a rockery built in 1905 filled with narrow passages and caves made entirely from imported stone. You'll also pass through extensive forest filled with towering century-old pines bordered by marshland and the vast but increasingly threatened Ipswich River ecosystem.

Start: Ipswich Audubon Headquarters
Nearest town: Topsfield
Distance: 2.7-mile multiloop trail
Approximate hiking time: 1.5 hours
Difficulty: Easy
Trail surface: Packed earth with some rock
Seasons: Year-round
Other trail users: Birders, swimmers, paddle sports enthusiasts, and snowshoers; no bicycles allowed
Canine compatibility: No dogs allowed

Land status: Private reservation open to nonmembers for a fee; no bikes allowed
Fees and permits: Trail-use fee
Schedule: Open dawn to dusk, Tues–Sun; closed Mon
Maps: Fold-up map given after paying admission
Trail contacts: Ipswich River Wildlife Sanctuary, (978) 887-9264; www.massaudubon.org/Nature _Connection/Sanctuaries/Ips wich_River/index.php; ipswich river@massaudubon.org

Finding the trailhead: Take exit 50 off I-95 to Route 1 and drive north toward Topsfield. After 3 miles, turn right (south) onto Route 97 and within less than 1 mile, turn left onto Perkins Row. Audubon entrance will be to your right marked with signage. GPS: N42 37.8964 / W70 55.2506

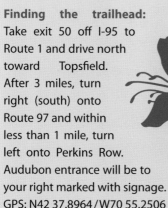

THE HIKE

Before hitting the trails, check in at the visitor center, a historic white house originally built by Governor Simon Bradstreet's grandson in 1763. In addition to paying the required admission fee here, you'll receive a trail map, and staff will share the latest information on animal sightings and trail conditions. Once off the visitor center front porch, turn right, following the Rockery sign, and pass between two red wooden buildings, straight ahead into a meadow. Here you may spot some bobolink or eastern bluebirds and tree swallows flittering around the nesting boxes that have been installed.

After departing this meadow and heading down through scrub brush, you'll be on the Innermost Trail. Soon the trail levels out into a large pine grove and then down a slope onto a boardwalk passing over a marshy area, where you have

Passing through a rockery tunnel

a great chance of spotting some waterfowl. Wetlands here have one of the largest concentrations of nesting wood ducks in Massachusetts. A viewing platform will be to your right as you continue on the boardwalk; a few steps before it ends, you'll reach a T intersection, where you want to turn left onto the Waterfowl Pond Trail. You are now on a traprock-covered trail surface since the trail bed is level with the marshland surrounding you. Straight ahead you'll see an arched stone bridge crossing a marsh onto a wooded island. This and the accompanying carriage roads were built at the turn of the century after the Audubon Society purchased the land from the Bradstreet family.

Once you cross this stone bridge, you'll have plenty of opportunities for viewing wildlife along a footpath loop that circles a small pond and is surrounded by benches and a wooden platform to your left. Evidence of beaver activity—tree stumps gnawed to points—is abundant along the pond shore as well. As soon as you turn left onto Averill's Island Loop Trail, pines tower overhead as you proceed on the boardwalk fringing the marsh. You'll have some good marsh views to your left before heading deep into a pine grove. Walking through these stately pines as breezes whisper through them is made all the more special with wide-open marsh visible through the trees, especially on a clear day with blue skies make a striking contrast.

Soon you'll get close-up views of the Ipswich River down an embankment through the trees to your right, providing an excellent overview of this winding body of water. Eight miles of this slow-moving river flow through the sanctuary. These waters can be explored with a canoe if you are a Mass Audubon member. After covering the entire Averill's Island Loop Trail, you'll realize that Averill's Island is really less of an island and more like a peninsula. You'll continue through hemlock up on a knoll paralleling marsh visible through the trees to your right, where you'll continue to see evidence of beaver chewings.

After turning right onto the Rockery Trail Loop, you'll soon be passing over a boardwalk heading out to a small pine island in the middle of the marsh. If in doubt, follow the green trail signs onto a pine-studded drumlin separating Rockery Pond to your left with the marsh to your right. You'll pass a gigantic cedar tree that looks as though it's from the Pacific Northwest at the pond's edge to your left, and shortly you'll begin to climb through the human-created Rockery. Huge boulders are mounded in various positions, creating caves, cliffs, and labyrinths to climb through and making it a great attraction for kids as well as kids at heart. As you're walking through, you'll see that you're on an "island of discovery." After climbing up a hill through mostly swamp maple over erosion bars built into the forest floor, you'll reach the field below the visitor center. Continue up through this meadow

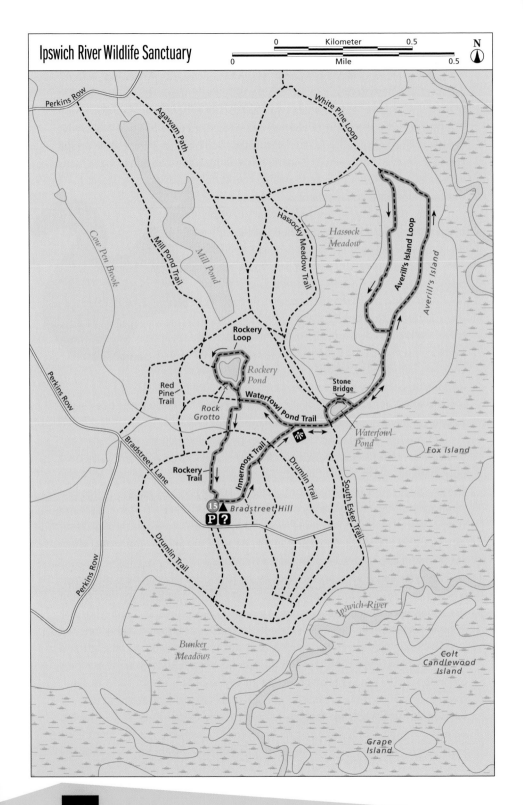

Ipswich River Wildlife Sanctuary

0 Kilometer 0.5
0 Mile 0.5

N

Perkins Row

Agawam Path

White Pine Loop

Cow Pen Brook

Mill Pond Trail

Mill Pond

Hassocky Meadow Trail

Hassock Meadow

Averill's Island Loop

Averill's Island

Rockery Loop

Rockery Pond

Red Pine Trail

Rock Grotto

Waterfowl Pond Trail

Stone Bridge

Waterfowl Pond

Fox Island

Perkins Row

Bradstreet Lane

Rockery Trail

Innermost Trail

Drumlin Trail

South Esker Trail

15

Bradstreet Hill

P ?

Perkins Row

Drumlin Trail

Bunker Meadows

Ipswich River

Colt Candlewood Island

Grape Island

on the trail bed, which now parallels the woods line, providing excellent habitat for scarlet tanagers, rose-breasted grosbeaks, and Baltimore orioles. Colorful wood warblers stop here to rest and feed during spring migration. You'll complete the loop as you head back between the red buildings to the parking area.

If you decide that you would like to become a member of the Massachusetts Audubon Society, you will get free statewide access to all Audubon trails as well as an accompanying guide and the monthly *Sanctuary* magazine.

MILES AND DIRECTIONS

0.0   After walking on a path from the parking lot up to a white historic house, which serves as the Audubon headquarters, turn left onto the trailhead.

0.1   Depart the meadow, heading down through scrub brush.

0.2   Turn left, continuing on the Innermost Trail, where you'll emerge out of scrub brush into a large pine grove.

0.3   Cross the Drumlin Trail and continue on Innermost Trail down a slope within the woods.

0.4   Pass a viewing platform to your right, continuing on a boardwalk.

0.5   Turn at a T intersection onto Averill's Island Loop Trail.

0.6   The deep pine forest noticeably opens up with the larger trees farther apart.

0.7   Enjoy your first view of the Ipswich River down an embankment through the trees to your right.

0.8   Continue northward on the Averill's Island Loop Trail (counterclockwise).

1.3   At end of loop turn right (south). Take the short loop northwest of Waterfowl Pond, crossing the Stone Bridge. Return to main trail by turning right.

1.75   Innermost Trail intersects from the left; continue straight (west) on Waterfowl Pond Trail.

2.0   Turn right to access the Rockery Loop counterclockwise. Pass a gigantic cedar tree that looks as though it's from the Pacific Northwest at the pond's edge to your left.

2.3   At end of Rockery Loop, continue straight back toward the start.

2.7   Complete the loop after retracing your steps back between the red barns to the parking area.

Appleton Farms Grass Rides

The name "Grass Rides" stems from this property's original function hosting carriage roads. The word "ride" comes from Europe to designate a path made for horseback riding. Horse-drawn carriages raced here in the late 1800s and early 1900s, which is why the main trails are remarkably level and wide, looping through thick forest. Appleton is considered to be the oldest farm in continuous operation in the United States; some plantings within these vast farmlands date back to 1638, when the town of Ipswich granted the land to Thomas Appleton. However, it was only relatively recently, in 1998, that Appleton Farms was opened to the public with an additional 4 miles of trails and community-supported agriculture.

Start: To the right of large map board with giveaway maps at the head of the parking lot

Nearest town: Hamilton

Distance: 3.4-mile cloverleaf

Approximate hiking time: 2.5 hours

Difficulty: Moderate

Trail surface: Packed earth, gravel access roads, grass

Seasons: Year-round

Other trail users: Cross-country skiers and snowshoers

Canine compatibility: Dogs allowed on Grass Rides trails but not in Appleton Farm fields

Land status: Trustees of Reservations property

Fees and permits: Donation requested at trailhead drop box

Schedule: 8:00 a.m. to sunset daily

Maps: On signboard and complimentary fold-up maps at trailhead

Trail contacts: Appleton Farms Grass Rides, Highland Street, Hamilton, MA 01982; (978) 356-5728; www.thetrustees.org

Finding the trailhead: From Route 128, take exit 20A to Route 1A and follow Route 1A north for approximately 7 miles. Turn left onto Waldingfield Road, past an Appleton Farms sign and parking area to your left. This is not the point of access for this hike. Continue down Waldingfield Road as it transitions to Goodhue Street and then intersects Highland Street. Turn left onto Highland and the parking area will be less than 0.5 mile to your left. GPS: N42 38.9629/W70 52.1722

THE HIKE

egin on a grassy lane through rolling meadows and rows of impressive maples flanking both sides of the trail bed. Upon turning left at a four-way intersection, you'll briefly pass through thick forest on a wide access road with a stone wall lining the left-hand side of the trail. You're heading northeast toward a loop around the Plains. You'll quickly emerge into expansive rolling meadows, following wheel-tracked farm roads periodically marked with green hiker symbol signs on a white background affixed to white posts. Much of the surrounding land is working farm with cattle grazing behind fences in the distance.

Once you turn right at a four-way intersection of farm roads, you'll notice that the route is marked by both horse and hiker symbols and a split rail fence wired with electricity to keep cattle in close by to your right. The roadbed here is level but can get muddy depending on the season. Proceed along the loop in a counterclockwise direction. Soon you'll pass a Kentucky gate to your right complete with a descriptive sign and diagram showing how you can open and close the gate without dismounting from your horse.

After passing this gate, you'll round a corner with a large stand of red pine to your left within the meadow. To your right, large expanses of field extend into the distance punctuated with large oaks, giving you wide-open views. You'll also pass

Farm road through the meadow with a line of maples on either side

133-acre Great Pasture, which supports one of New England's largest populations of bobolinks and meadowlarks.

Pass Briar Hill, and turn left at a three-way intersection, continuing on a well-graded sand and gravel private road able to accommodate any type of vehicle. A large pine grove borders this intersection straight ahead. Follow this road until you

The Kentucky Gate

Inventor William D. Miller of Raywick, Kentucky, developed the "Kentucky gate" in March 1915. This unique design enables riders to open and close the gate from either side of the fence without dismounting. The counterweight mechanism is the key behind this innovation. This last surviving Kentucky Gate on Appleton Farms was completely restored as a community service project during the summer of 2001 by members of the Hamilton-Wenham and the Ipswich Rotary Clubs.

Stone pillar that once adorned Gore Hall at Harvard University

round a corner and cut to the left at a little white sign with black lettering onto a grassy footpath at the edge of a field. You'll pass a series of stone steps to your right, which lead to a private residence.

You'll soon pass a small pond directly to your right (at about 10 o'clock on the loop) and then reconnect with the four-way farm road intersection that you previously passed through. Before retracing your steps straight ahead, you'll see a stone plaque at the end of the stone wall to your right dedicated in memory of Leo Ramella (1923–2007), who lived with his family in the red cottage visible off to the right through the field and tended these farmlands for more than fifty years.

As soon as you cross back through the stone wall into the woods, turn left up a steep hill with the stone wall separating the meadows from woods now close by to your left along with deep pine forest to your right. You're heading southeast on the second loop, walking clockwise. You'll know that you've reached the top of Pigeon Hill when off in the field to your left you see a tribute to the alma mater for generations of Appletons, a stone pillar that once adorned Gore Hall at Harvard University.

Follow the path as it curves inward away from the meadow, and pass straight ahead through a clearing onto a carriage road, which then curves sharply to the right, carved into the side of a hill overlooking a wooded marsh down through the trees to your left. Next continue straight through a four-way intersection, and then approach a T intersection on this wide flat wood road surrounded by a mix of pine and deciduous trees. Before reaching the T, curve to the right, return-ing to the four-way intersection that you first encountered on this route.

Appleton: A Working Farm

It all started when Samuel Appleton established the farm back in 1636 for subsistence crops like corn and hay. Later generations harvested timber from the land leaving vast open meadows to support cattle. The farm's activities evolved in a different direction toward the end of the nineteenth century, serving as a country estate complete with foxhunts and steeplechases. The farm is today one of the oldest continuously operating farms in the country after being maintained by nine generations of the Appleton family. Thanks to the Trustees of Reservations' preservation efforts, the land remains a working farm with a dairy and a Community-Supported Agriculture Program that pro-vides farm-fresh produce to shareholders.

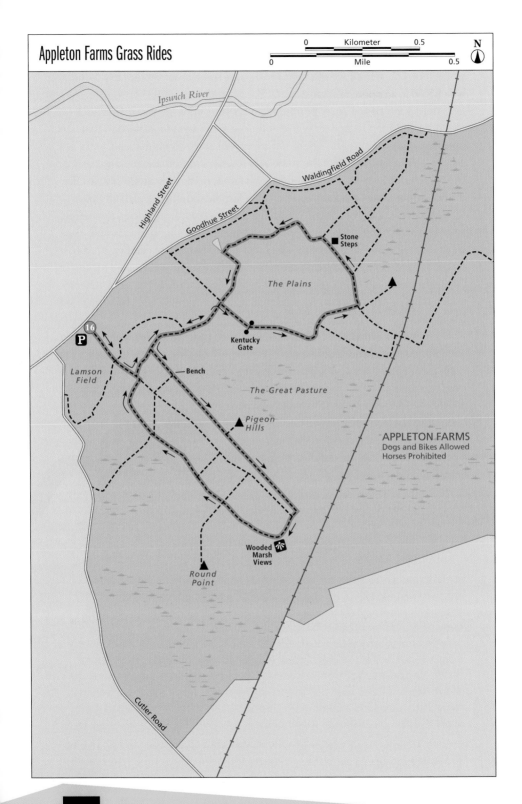

Appleton Farms Grass Rides

0 Kilometer 0.5

0 Mile 0.5

N

Ipswich River

Highland Street

Goodhue Street

Waldingfield Road

Stone Steps

The Plains

Kentucky Gate

P 16

Lamson Field

Bench

The Great Pasture

Pigeon Hills

APPLETON FARMS
Dogs and Bikes Allowed
Horses Prohibited

Wooded Marsh Views

Round Point

Cutler Road

MILES AND DIRECTIONS

0.0 Begin in an open meadow passing between rows of large maples on either side of the trail.

0.1 Turn left at a four-way intersection, and there will be a stone wall lining the left-hand side of the trail.

0.2 Emerge into farm fields and follow the marked farm road outlined by wheel tracks.

0.5 Reach the beginning of the northern loop, and turn right at a four-way intersection of farm roads within these fields.

0.6 Pass a Kentucky gate to your right.

0.8 You'll pass a sign for the Great Pasture featuring a timeline of what happened here from 1930 to 1934.

1.0 Turn left (northwest) at a three-way intersection, continuing on a well-graded gravel and sand private road.

1.1 Cut to the left at a little white sign with black lettering onto a grassy footpath off the private road.

1.2 Pass a series of stone steps to your right climbing up above the trail bed.

1.3 Turn left (southwest) onto a grassy farm road back out into open meadow surrounded by huge maples.

1.4 Reach a split in the trail and veer to the left, heading out of the dense pine into a lighter wooded cover with clusters of small pine to your right.

1.5 Pass a small pond directly to your right in a field just before sharply turning to the left, continuing to follow the farm road.

1.6 Complete this northern loop and continue straight on the farm road between the loops.

1.8 Immediately after passing back through the stone wall into the woods, start the southern loop by turning left up a hill on a footpath with the meadows below through the trees to your left.

2.0 Pass a clearing overlooking the meadows below complete with a bench, then continue on the wooded footpath straight ahead into thick pine forest.

2.1 After passing through a deep mix of hemlock and pine, the forest canopy noticeably opens up, making it lighter.

2.2 Reach the top of Pigeon Hill marked with a signboard describing the Great Pasture down below to your left.

2.3 Continue straight past a wood road to your right, continuing on the footpath paralleling the stone walls and meadow to your left.

2.5 Curve inward (right) away from the meadow, pass through a clearing, then continue straight ahead onto a wood road.

2.6 Get your first glimpses of wooded marsh down a hill through the woods to your left while being surrounded by a mixed forest of pine and various deciduous trees.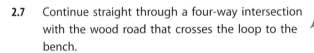

2.7 Continue straight through a four-way intersection with the wood road that crosses the loop to the bench.

2.9 Curve right (northeast) through a T intersection on a wide flat wood road surrounded by a mix of pine and deciduous growth.

3.3 Complete the loop after returning to the four-way intersection that you first confronted on this route and turn left.

3.4 Reach the parking lot after retracing your steps on the farm road through the meadow.

Ravenswood Park

Much of this route winds through and alongside a vast magnolia swamp along with some spectacular ridge lines punctuated with interesting rock formations and some kettle holes and ponds. You'll also get to see the spot where the Hermit of Gloucester, Mason A. Walton, built his cabin in 1884 and studied nature in these woods. Based on these experiences, he wrote several books, including A Hermit's Wild Friends.

Start: Cape Ann Discovery Center parking lot off Route 127
Nearest town: Gloucester
Distance: 3.1-mile lollipop
Approximate hiking time: 2 hours
Difficulty: Easy
Trail surface: Packed earth and gravel, boardwalks, some rock
Seasons: Year-round
Other trail users: Birders, snowshoers, cross-country skiers
Canine compatibility: Dogs allowed

Land status: Trustees of Reservations property
Fees and permits: No fee but donations appreciated in Discovery Center
Schedule: Open dawn to dusk daily
Maps: Signboard with complimentary fold-up maps at trailhead
Trail contacts: Trustees of Reservations, (978) 526-8687; www .thetrustees.org; neregion@ttor.org

Finding the trailhead: Take exit 14 off Route 128 to Route 133. Follow Route 133 east for 3 miles and then turn right onto Route 127 South. Sign and parking area will be to your right in approximately 2 miles. GPS: N42 35.4987 / W70 41.9183

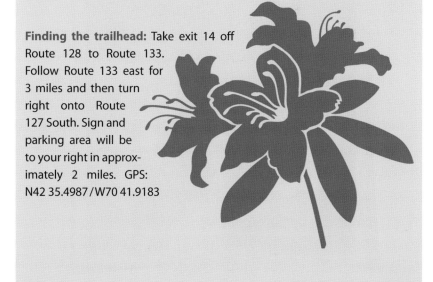

From the back of the Cape Ann Discovery Center parking lot off Route 127, you'll pass a map board to your right onto a level graded access road with boulders on either side. Here this dirt road passes through mostly oak and ash. Starting here and throughout the route, you'll notice a large number of erratics, boulders left behind by glaciers of long ago, punctuating the forest floor. Upon turning left onto the Magnolia Swamp Trail, you are now suddenly on a narrow footpath bordered by a row of stones on either side beneath thick hemlock. The trail bed is rugged and stony up on a ridge within the woods. Soon you'll be surrounded by oak and pine, and you'll pass a boulder the size of a car precariously perched on top of this ridge courtesy of prehistoric glacial action. The trail curves behind this bolder back onto the forest floor, continuing to traverse rocky terrain.

Ledge Hill Trail bed

You'll transition into mountain laurel surrounding the trail while continuing to follow a ridgeline elevated above the rest of the forest floor. Treed vistas within the forest to your right make this stretch intriguing. Cross another trail, continuing straight on the Magnolia Trail, and soon you'll cross a wooden-planked elevated walkway above Magnolia Swamp surrounded by mostly swamp maples. These two planks extend for a good distance until a few paces after departing this boardwalk. Then you'll be on a level yet rocky and rugged trail bed and pass a depression to your left surrounded by boulders strewn across the forest floor.

What is now a footpath is carved into the side of a hill within the rugged forest overlooking a vast wooded marsh called Great Magnolia Swamp, populated by the endangered sweetbay magnolia, directly down to your right. You'll enter another boardwalk jutting out into Magnolia Swamp for a short stretch before curving back to the solid footpath once again. You'll notice that sections of swamp to your right are protected by a metal grid fence although it's unclear why somebody would want to wade into the muddy swamp to disturb it. Once you reach an intersection, where you'll see a narrow wooden boardwalk heading back across the Magnolia Swamp, turn right, cross over on this walkway, and curve up a hill away from the swamp, passing through mostly pine forest interspersed with some oak and laurel.

Once you are again on Old Salem Road, you'll be traversing a wide, open level gravel access road rather than a narrow footpath. The forest floor on either side remains rugged but is farther removed and doesn't impact the trail bed. You'll reach a plaque to your left commemorating where the hermit of Gloucester lived in a cabin in this vicinity for thirty-three years. He originally settled here to cure his tuberculosis but stayed long after recuperating, studying nature and sharing his findings with the locals.

A few steps beyond this site you'll reach another trail intersection, where you want to turn right onto the Evergreen Road, which is marked with another small brown sign with white lettering. After passing through intersections and making turns in rapid succession, you'll steadily climb up across a ledge on the forest floor until you reach the Ledge Hill Trail. Be sure to turn left onto this trail for a brief stretch, reaching an overlook outfitted with a bench, where you can enjoy views of Gloucester Harbor below. It's now clearly apparent just how close you are to the ocean. Retrace your steps and continue back onto the Ledge Hill Trail. From here

🌱 **Green Tip:**
Even if it claims to be biodegradable,
don't put soap into streams or lakes.
If you need to use soap, bring the water to you.

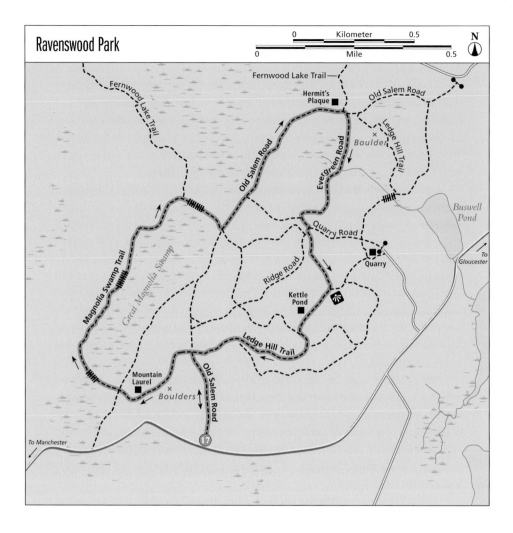

Ravenswood Park

0   Kilometer   0.5
0   Mile   0.5
N

Fernwood Lake Trail
Fernwood Lake Trail
Hermit's Plaque
Old Salem Road
Old Salem Road
Evergreen Road
× Boulder
Ledge Hill Trail
Buswell Pond
To Gloucester
Quarry Road
Quarry
Magnolia Swamp Trail
Great Magnolia Swamp
Ridge Road
Kettle Pond
Ledge Hill Trail
Mountain Laurel
× Boulders
Old Salem Road
To Manchester
17

you'll be traveling along rugged rock ridge with harbor activity such as boat horns audible through the forest. You'll see a kettle pond down through the trees to your right, the remainder of glacial ice chunks that melted into the ground, leaving a depression. Here you'll have a good overview of this geological formation along with the surrounding forest pocked with boulders.

Throughout this vicinity, the trail bed itself is at times solid rock and is mostly flanked with stones forming a rough stone wall on either side of this narrow passage. Even though the trail heads up and down numerous hills, a sustained climb isn't encountered. You'll complete the loop back at the intersection where you previously turned onto the Magnolia Swamp Trail.

MILES AND DIRECTIONS

0.0 Begin at the green metal gate straight ahead to the back of the Discovery Center parking area.

0.2 Turn left at the little green sign with white lettering pointing to the Magnolia Swamp Trail.

0.3 Pass a boulder the size of a car precariously perched on top of a ridge.

0.4 Transition into mountain laurel surrounding the trail while traversing a ridge.

0.5 Pass straight through a trail intersection, continuing on the Magnolia Trail.

0.6 Depart a wood-planked elevated walkway.

0.7 Enter another boardwalk jutting out into the wooded marsh for a short stretch.

1.2 Turn right at a trail intersection onto a narrow wooden boardwalk back across the Magnolia Swamp.

1.3 Turn left at a T intersection onto Old Salem Road.

1.4 Continue straight through an intersection on Old Salem Road marked with a small brown sign with white lettering.

1.5 Descend gradually and then level out with a wooded swamp close by to your left.

1.7 Begin ascending a series of hills up into the woods.

1.7 Reach a plaque to your left commemorating the Hermit of Gloucester.

2.2 Turn left onto Quarry Road and within ten steps turn left onto a footpath.

2.4 Intersect the Ledge Hill Trail and turn left, progressing a few paces to a bench and an overlook of Gloucester Harbor below.

2.5 View a kettle pond down through the trees to your right.

3.1 After looping back to the Magnolia Swamp Trail intersection, turn left and retrace your steps back to the parking lot.

Lynn Woods Reservation

Considered to be the second largest municipal park in the United States, Lynn Woods Reservation, a 2,200-acre forest park, was founded in 1881 and offers over 30 miles of scenic trails to explore. Even more remarkable is that this vast, open space feels like a downright wilderness at times even though it's surrounded by dense suburban development.

Start: From the Kiwanis Special Needs Kids Camp sign at the head of the parking lot at the top of the hill, follow a paved driveway

Nearest town: Lynn

Distance: 3.4-mile double loop

Approximate hiking time: 2.5 hours

Difficulty: Moderate

Trail surface: Packed earth with some rock

Seasons: Year-round

Other trail users: Birders, snowshoers

Canine compatibility: Dogs on leash allowed

Land status: City of Lynn

Fees and permits: None

Schedule: Sunrise to sunset daily

Maps: Available from the Friends of Lynn Woods at www.flw.org /pdf_files/lwmap.pdf

Trail contacts: Lynn Department of Public Works, 250 Commercial Street, Lynn, MA 01905; (781) 477-7099; LynnWoodsRanger@aol.com

Finding the trailhead: From US 1 North, take the Walnut Street exit in Saugus, following this street east into the town of Lynn. After 2 miles, at a blinking light turn left onto Pennybrook Road. Follow Pennybrook Road to the end, reaching the parking area. GPS: N42 28.6121 / W70 59.22

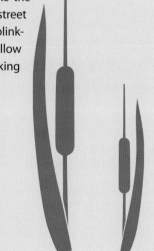

THE HIKE

After following a paved driveway up through to the back of a Kiwanis Special Needs Kids Camp, curve around to a cul-de-sac at the back of the campgrounds, where you'll see a brown Lynn Woods sign with a green gate. Continue past the gate, paralleling a wooden guardrail close by to your left until you reach two large boulders. Pass around these stones onto a well-worn footpath, which soon transitions into a green-blazed access road.

You'll be increasingly climbing through a mix of small pine, medium oak, and white birch. New growth is particularly prominent in this area to your right as the trail surface is mostly rock ledge. The road soon levels out into a grassy clearing before continuing to curve up to the right over a surface that's rocky at different intervals. You'll notice a rock ridge to your right as you're progressing before reaching another intersection, where you'll continue straight, descending off the ridge down through small white birch clustered to your left along with larger oak and pine to your right.

Continue following the green markings as you split off to the left on a worn footpath surrounded by wild blueberry bushes and small oak saplings. You'll continue on rugged terrain through several more intersections before turning left onto an orange-blazed trail marked with a Dungeon Rock sign. From this point, a level and wide-open trail surface makes it a pleasant amble through the forest. Keep your eyes open for golden crowned kinglets and hooded warblers. You'll soon split

View of Boston skyline from atop Mount Gilead

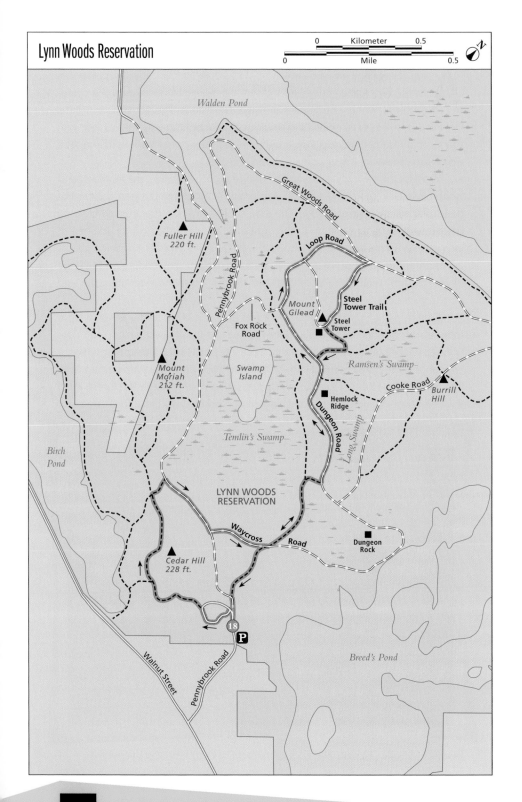

Walden Pond

Great Woods Road

Fuller Hill
220 ft.

Loop Road

Pennybrook Road

**Steel
Tower Trail**

Fox Rock
Road

Mount
Gilead

Steel
Tower

Ramsen's Swamp

Swamp
Island

Mount
Moriah
212 ft.

Cooke Road

Burrill
Hill

Hemlock
Ridge

Long Swamp

Temlin's Swamp

Dungeon Road

Birch
Pond

LYNN WOODS
RESERVATION

Waycross   Road

Dungeon
Rock

Cedar Hill
228 ft.

18 P

Walnut Street

Pennybrook Road

Breed's Pond

0   Kilometer   0.5
0   Mile   0.5

N

off to the left back onto a green-blazed footpath, which is a fraction of the width of the access road but still with a sand and gravel surface, passing through mostly deciduous down a hill within the woods.

Once you're on a wide, flat gravel access road traversing a ridge within the forest, you'll pass a sign to your right up on a tree that reads HEMLOCK RIDGE. As you round this corner, you'll notice that many of the larger hemlock are mostly dead. If you look off to your left down an embankment, you'll notice that you're traversing rugged terrain, but thanks to the well-graded roadbed, you're doing it effortlessly. Eventually the road heads downward, where you'll cross a stream and you'll occasionally see orange blazes on the surrounding trees paralleling this road. You are now completely level and will remain this way on the Dungeon Road Trail until you dead-end at a T intersection, where you'll turn right and make another immediate right onto the Loop Road Steel Tower Trail.

What's In a Trail Name?

Hiking through Lynn Woods takes you through a maze of old carriage roads and footpaths. Without a map, GPS, or the kindness of strangers, it's very easy to get lost. This is in spite of the fact that the trail names are well marked and some of them are downright intriguing. One is a well-graded, centuries-old cart road called Pennybrook Road. Built for draft animals to haul out timber, this wide road gradually descends toward a fieldstone bridge spanning a stream. Long ago, all who crossed here were charged a toll of one penny.

Another sign you'll see on this route is one pointing to Dungeon Rock via Dungeon Road. Historical accounts tell us that in 1658, British soldiers captured four pirate buccaneers who came ashore on the Saugus River. Three were captured and hung but the fourth, Thomas Veal, escaped into the woods. It was believed that he took a hoard of stolen booty with him as he headed deeper and deeper into the woods, finally arriving at a natural cave in what is now Lynn Woods. One day an earthquake unlodged a gigantic piece of the rock, permanently sealing Veal inside. Over the years, many have tried in vain to locate the treasure.

After gradually yet steadily climbing, you'll reach what was once a steel fire tower on the peak of Mount Gilead. The top of this tower is no longer intact, but the steel staircase, although not extending to the ground, is still there. You'll be high up on a ridge and have some clear views of the Boston skyline, making the journey up to this point all the more worthwhile. Cut down on a footpath winding to the left side of this ridge, intersecting back with the Dungeon Road Trail. From here, turn left, retracing your steps back on the orange and then green blazes. Toward the end of the route, you'll immediately pass through a pine grove with needles blanketing the trail as soon as you cross the orange trail. Continue down through the woods on a footpath with small oak on either side until you reach a T intersection, where you'll turn left, pass around a green metal gate, and return to the parking lot.

MILES AND DIRECTIONS

0.0   From the asphalt parking lot at the top of the hill, follow a paved driveway leading up through a kids' camp.

0.1   Pass around two large boulders onto a well-worn footpath.

0.3   Curve to the right at a split in the trail where you'll see a B73 marker up on a tree along with a green marker on a tree to your left.

0.4   Continue straight, now descending off the ridge, at an intersection marked with a B75 sign up on a large oak tree.

0.5   Turn right onto Waycross Road, an access road, at a wide intersection.

0.7   Turn left onto an orange-blazed trail where you'll see a sign on a tree marking Dungeon Rock.

0.9   Split to the left onto a green-blazed footpath also marked with a small white C72 sign with black lettering.

1.2   Continue straight at another intersection where you'll see a rock outcropping through the trees ahead.

1.4   Pass a sign to your right up on a tree marking Hemlock Ridge.

1.7   Continue straight on the orange-blazed Dungeon Road. Pass Fox Rock Road on your left.

2.1   Turn right at a trail intersection and make another immediate sharp right onto the Loop Road Steel Tower Trail.

2.3   Reach the steel tower and overlook.

2.4   Reconnect with Dungeon Road after cutting down on a footpath winding to the left side of the ridge.

3.0   Turn left at a T intersection, crossing Waycross Road and heading back to a main access road, where you'll see a green gate in the distance.

3.4   Pass around a green metal gate, returning to the parking lot.

Minute Man National Historical Park: Battle Road Trail

This route covers the more wooded section of the Battle Road Trail as well as many key historic landmarks along this route taken by minutemen battling the redcoats from Lexington to Concord. At different points you'll notice that the old battle road-bed parallels modern secondary roads such as Route 2A. It's clear that these more modern byways rely on the same natural contours utilized centuries ago.

Start: Merriam Corner parking lot trailhead
Nearest town: Concord
Distance: 3.9 miles one way
Approximate hiking time: 3 hours one way
Difficulty: Easy
Trail surface: Packed gravel and pavement
Seasons: Year-round
Other trail users: Bikers, birders
Canine compatibility: Dogs allowed on leash no longer than 6 feet long. Must clean up after.
Land status: National Park Service
Fees and permits: None
Schedule: Sunrise to sunset daily
Maps: Available at visitor center and online at www.nps.gov/mima/upload/MIMA%20Park%20Map.pdf
Trail contacts: Minute Man National Historical Park, 174 Liberty Street, Concord, MA 01742; (978) 369-6993

Finding the trailhead: From I-95, take exit 29B and then follow 2 W (Cambridge Turnpike). Parking area marked with signage will be 3.6 miles to your right. To arrange a shuttle, leave one car in the Visitor Center parking lot approximately 2 miles down Route 2A. GPS: N42 27.5316/W71 19.3268

THE HIKE

his route covers a segment of the Battle Road beginning at Merriam Corner, the Battle Road's westernmost point, and ending at the visitor center. It can either be an out-and-back occupying the better part of a day or, if hiking with others, can be one way if you park a car at both ends.

Considering that battles took place in 1775 along this route, the Minute Man National Historical Park was established startlingly recently by an act of Congress in 1959. And not a moment too soon, as you'll see that residential development has encroached very closely on numerous segments of the Battle Road. Here you'll literally walk in the footsteps of Patriots like Paul Revere who fought for freedom from Lexington to Concord, igniting the American Revolution. Beyond the battlefields, the trail's interpretive signage examines other cultural developments and how they shaped the landscape over time.

Begin by crossing a wooden plank walkway over marshland and entering a wide-open field with Route 2A in the distance to your right. Up ahead alongside the trail to your right overlooking this meadow, an illustrative signboard indicates that this grassland dates back to the seventeenth century, hosting some of the Revolutionary War's first skirmishes.

Upon reaching Brooks Hill, location of another successful Patriot ambush, you'll also see an interpretive signboard spotlighting the various tradesmen, like

Boardwalk Section of Battle Road Trail

blacksmiths and farmers, who surrounded this road during the Revolutionary War. The next battle site you'll encounter is the Bloody Angle. It is here that colonists spotted the British approaching as they hid behind stone walls and were able to ambush them due to the angle at which they were situated.

After cutting through a field with stone walls topped with split rails off to your right, you'll pass through a stone wall and continue on the Battle Road flanked by well-formed stone walls and large maples on either side for as far as the eye can see until you reach a wide-open meadow where the historic Captain William Smithhouse sits high up on a hill to your left. Captain Smith was commander of the Lincoln Minute Men on April 19, 1775. You'll pass it up close to your left and see how beautifully intact it is, making it stand out from other home sites that are merely stone footprints.

Living History on the Battle Road

Without a doubt, the primary attraction of this dirt and gravel road is being able to walk the same path taken by colonial militia and minutemen who clashed with British troops in 1775 led by General Thomas Gage. But it's the civilian life that existed at the same time along this battle road that gives the history lesson a richer context. At Brooks Hill and its vicinity, for instance, you'll pass an interpretive signboard describing blacksmiths and farmers who kept the militia provisioned during battle. Another illustrative plaque commemorates a historic hay meadow down below. These marshy grasslands were drained and used not only as battlefields, but the rich, moist soil was perfect for growing hay.

After emerging in an open meadow, the trail bed gradually slopes downward toward a corrugated metal tunnel where you'll pass under a paved road. Upon exiting, you'll gradually climb up and away through the meadow and then curve into a wooded knoll overlooking a housing development down to your left. This segment provides a clear example of the juxtaposition of modern-day residential development along with the road noise of 2A nearby with such a treasured historic landmark.

After passing through another meadow on a stone dust surface, you'll reach a monument with a metal placard embedded in stone along with a descriptive signboard marking the spot where Paul Revere was captured. Shortly you'll be on a wide access road passing the Josiah Nelson home site to your left; it's nothing more than several square foundation stones embedded in the earth. Legend has it that Josiah was the first casualty of the American Revolution, merely by inadvertently asking a British general if the redcoats were coming.

Minute Man National Historical Park–Battle Road Trail

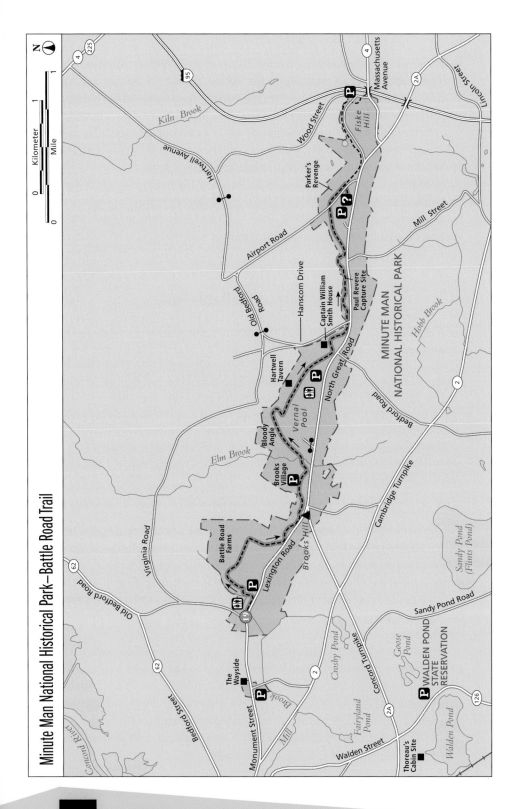

After crossing a paved road, continue on the trail, which is clearly marked with a granite pillar on either side spanned by heavy gauge chain, reaching Parkers Revenge. Here, a display board with map and illustration depict this battle showing how the view looked in 1775 from this vantage point. Some faint similarities remain, but it's mostly unrecognizable. You'll soon turn right, exiting the Battle Road, pass the visitor center to your right, and reach the parking lot, where you'll be standing beside a circular stone wall and a detailed map board. From here you can either retrace your steps, doubling back, or drive back to Merriam Corner.

MILES AND DIRECTIONS

0.0   Begin at the Merriam Corner parking lot, the western-most point on the Battle Road.

0.3   Depart a field heading under the cover of some large pine with an overgrown field continuing to your left.

0.5   Pass a signboard to the left marking historic farmland as the trail bed straddles a field on either side.

0.8   Begin crossing a long wooden planked boardwalk elevated over a marshy area.

1.0   Pass the Brooks Hill Battle Site, the scene of a successful Patriot ambush on the redcoats.

1.2   Pass a signboard marking the Bloody Angle.

1.4   Pass a sign discussing the various trades that surrounded the road during the Revolutionary War.

1.5   A signboard to the left of the trail marks a historic hay meadow.

1.7   Begin cutting through a field with stone walls topped with split rails off to your right.

> 🍃 **Green Tip:**
> *Consider citronella as an effective natural mosquito repellent.*

1.8   Pass through a stone wall and turn right, continuing on the Battle Road flanked by well-formed stone walls on either side. You'll quickly turn left at another intersection, continuing on this road, which is wide and flat.

2.5   The Captain William Smith house comes into view to your left.

2.6   Cross a small stream.

2.8   Enter a tunnel with corrugated metal walls passing under a paved road above.

3.0   Reach a metal placard embedded in stone along with a descriptive signboard marking the spot where Paul Revere was captured.

3.3   Pass the Josiah Nelson home site, nothing more than several square foundation stones embedded in the earth.

3.5   Pass the Thomas Nelson home site to your right, now reduced to a roughly formed old stone foundation.

3.6   Reach Parkers Revenge.

3.7   Cross a paved road and walk through a stone wall, continuing on the Battle Road.

3.8   Pass the visitor center to your right, continuing straight on the path through scrubby cedar and oak.

3.9   Reach the end of the route at a circular stone wall and pick up your car. **(Option:** Retrace your steps for an out-and-back hike of 7.8 miles and finish at the trailhead.)

Walden Pond State Reservation

Hiking doesn't get any more straightforward or literary than circling 102-foot-deep Walden Pond in the very steps of Henry David Thoreau. This glacial kettle-hole pond is surrounded by Walden Woods, a vast, 2,680-acre tract of preserved forest land. So close to civilization in today's world, it still truly feels like you're in the middle of nowhere once you're on the trail. Thoreau's cabin site is now merely an outline of what is the birthplace of America's Back-to-the-Land Movement.

Start: Walden Pond State Reservation parking lot

Nearest town: Concord

Distance: 1.8-mile loop

Approximate hiking time: 1.5 hours

Difficulty: Easy

Trail surface: Packed earth with some rock

Seasons: Year-round

Other trail users: Birders, anglers, swimmers, paddlers, and snowshoers

Canine compatibility: No dogs allowed

Land status: State Department of Conservation and Recreation

Fees and permits: Parking fee per day

Schedule: Sunrise to sunset daily

Maps: On signboard at trailhead, available for purchase at gift shop, and online at www.mass.info /images/parks/walden_pond _state_reservation_trail_map.gif.

Trail contacts: Department of Conservation and Recreation, 251 Causeway Street, Suite 600, Boston, MA 02114-2104; (617) 626-1250

Finding the trailhead: From Route 128, take the exit for Route 2. In approximately 0.25 mile after you pass a Mobil gas station to your right, turn left onto Route 126. A sign marking the Walden Pond State Reservation parking lot will be to your left in 0.25 mile. GPS: N42 26.4575 / W71 20.0757

THE HIKE

From the split rail fence at the head of the parking lot, proceed past both a large map board and signboard, crossing Route 126 using the pedestrian crosswalk. You'll see the pond ahead down through the trees and a sign to your right stating WELCOME TO WALDEN POND STATE RESERVATION. Starting off on a wide footpath, you'll be close to the water's edge, which is down a small yet steep embankment to your left and protected with barbed wire at different intervals. A well-formed stone wall held together by concrete separates the path's right edge from the woods. You'll have water views through the cover of ash, oak, and some large pine as you progress. Soon the trail transitions to walking along a sandy shore next to the water. This is the first but not the last time in the route that you won't be physically separated from the water's edge. You'll notice the sudden change to more natural unimpeded surroundings. The shoreline walk is short, and quickly you'll be up above the water again. This time the path is narrower and flanked with barbed wire on each side. This has been installed to prevent people from straying away from the trail in either direction, causing erosion. However, stone steps lead down the steep bank to your left to the water's edge at different intervals, providing easy access to the water.

You'll reach a good vantage point overlooking Walden Pond where some well-established stone steps lead down to the water's edge as well as up into the

Thoreau Cabin Site

woods through large pine mixed with gnarly oak to your right. Once you approach a little brown sign with white lettering to your right pointing to the Thoreau House Site, climb up a short trail spur through mostly white pine leading up to a clearing where you see the original cabin foundation pattern marked with granite pillars spanned with chain. The foundation no longer exists, but a detailed signboard indicates that the ground was archaeologically excavated back in 1947, revealing the homestead's true location. Medium oak and stately pine surround this flat, peaceful clearing, and if you look back in the direction of where you entered, you can see the pond through the trees.

Henry David Thoreau's Repose

Henry David Thoreau lived at Walden Pond from July 1845 to September 1847. His experience at Walden provided the material for the book *Walden*, which is credited with helping to inspire awareness and respect for the natural environment. Because of Thoreau's legacy, Walden Pond has been designated a National Historic Landmark and is considered the birthplace of the conservation movement.

Thoreau admired Ralph Waldo Emerson's 1836 essay, "Nature," which advanced the concept of American Romanticism, that each individual should seek a spiritually fulfilling relationship with the natural world.

Grieving over the loss of his brother, Thoreau decided he wanted to pursue a career as a writer. When Emerson, a close friend and fellow Concord resident, offered him the use of a newly purchased woodlot at Walden Pond, Thoreau eagerly accepted and went to live and work near its shores in a rustic cabin. He kept a journal of his thoughts and his encounters with nature and society. Over the next few years, Thoreau wrote and rewrote (seven drafts in all) *Walden; or Life in the Woods,* one of the most famous works in American literature, which was published in 1854.

Continuing with the pond shore to your left, you'll at times have clear water views unobstructed by trees. It's difficult to believe that many of the large pines towering overhead didn't witness Thoreau's travails. This is due to the fact that all the trees surrounding Walden Pond were leveled during the hurricane of 1938. Just after you climb a series of stone steps high up above the pond with active train tracks close by to your right, you'll be up on a ridge with mostly pine and hemlock.

Once the trail curves down to the pond again, you'll encounter pockets of solitude that Thoreau may have experienced at the water's edge. After passing through

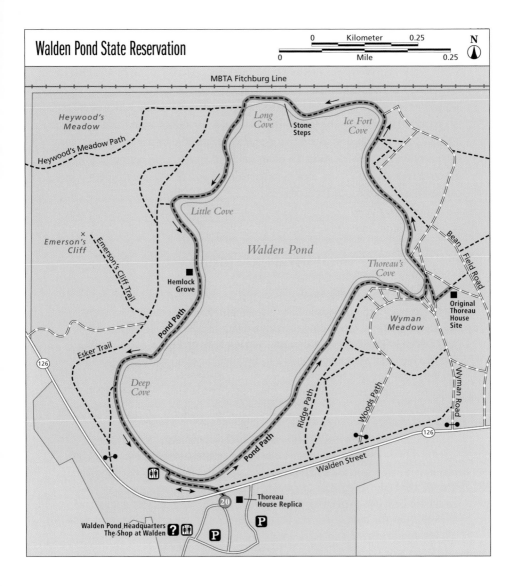

Kilometer

0   0.25

Mile

0   0.25

N

MBTA Fitchburg Line

Heywood's
Meadow

Heywood's Meadow Path

Long
Cove

Stone
Steps

Ice Fort
Cove

Little Cove

Walden Pond

Bean Field Road

Emerson's
Cliff

Emerson's Cliff Trail

Hemlock
Grove

Thoreau's
Cove

Original
Thoreau
House
Site

Pond Path

Wyman
Meadow

Esker Trail

Deep
Cove

Ridge Path

Woods Path

Wyman Road

126

126

Pond Path

Walden Street

126

Thoreau
House Replica

P

20

P

Walden Pond Headquarters
The Shop at Walden

P

a thick hemlock grove, you'll soon reach a boat launch area limited to paddle sports since motorized vessels aren't allowed on the pond. Continue close along the pond shore toward a stone wall at the water's edge. Soon, this wall serves as the trail bed where you'll be walking on top of it with the wide-open water directly below until you reach a sandy beach area down to your left with the visitor center and gift shop up to your right. This marks where you have completed the loop. Retrace your steps back up the access road and cross Route 126 back to the parking area.

MILES AND DIRECTIONS

0.0   Begin at the trailhead at Walden Pond State Reservation parking area.

0.1   Turn right off the road and onto a wide footpath close to the water's edge.

0.4   Reach a good vantage point of Walden Pond.

0.5   Turn right at a little brown sign with white lettering pointing up a short spur trail to the Thoreau House Site.

0.6   Curve to the left through a trail intersection continuing to closely parallel the pond shore down to your left.

0.8   Finish climbing a series of stone steps high up above the pond shore to your left with active train tracks to your right.

0.9   Turn left at another trail intersection heading down closer to the pond shore, which is visible through the trees.

1.3   Make a striking entrance into a hemlock grove that shrouds the trail's rugged surroundings.

1.5   Reach a boat launch providing access to Walden Pond's waters; activities are restricted to non-motorized water sports.

1.7   Turn right up away from the pond, retracing your steps on an access road.

1.8   After you cross Route 126, arrive back at the trailhead parking lot.

> 🌿 **Green Tip:**
> *When hiking in a group, walk single file on established trails to avoid widening them. If you come upon a sensitive area, spread out so you don't cut one path through the landscape. Don't create new trails where there were none before.*

Mount Misery Loop

Part of the Town of Lincoln's Conservation Land right off Route 117, this trail connects with Walden Pond. It was also a familiar stomping ground for Henry David Thoreau. Contrary to its severe name, Mount Misery is more of a hill than a mountain and reportedly received its name when two yoked oxen wandered here in the late 1700s and wrapped themselves around a tree, where they perished. Walking the trail today is anything but misery: It features terrain ranging from deep pine forest to picturesque views of the Sudbury River flanked with marsh teeming with bird life.

Start: Town of Lincoln Conservation Land parking lot
Nearest town: Lincoln
Distance: 1.6-mile loop
Approximate hiking time: 1.5 hours
Difficulty: Easy
Trail surface: Packed earth, rock, some gravel
Seasons: Year-round
Other trail users: Birders, snowshoers
Canine compatibility: Dogs permitted

Land status: Town of Lincoln Conservation Department
Fees and permits: No charge
Schedule: Dawn to dusk daily
Maps: On signboard at trailhead and available for purchase at www.lincolnconservation.org /LLCTBooksandMaps.html
Trail contacts: Lincoln Conservation Committee, Town Offices, Lincoln, MA 01773; (781) 259-2612; www.lincolntown.org

Finding the trailhead: Take exit 26 from Route 128 onto Route 20 east. Turn onto Route 117 West and follow approximately 7 miles to the Lincoln Conservation Land–Mount Misery parking entrance to your right. GPS: N42 25.0621 / W71 21.1931

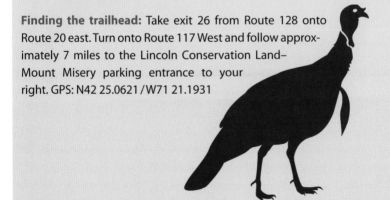

THE HIKE

From the parking lot marked with a brown sign with white lettering indicating that this is Town of Lincoln Conservation Land, pass through the split rail fence to the far right of the lot as your back is facing Route 117. The trail bed here is completely level; within a few steps, you'll see a signboard to your right containing a detailed trail map along with descriptions of local flora and fauna like skunk cabbage and raccoon. You'll soon cross a spillway made of stone and emptying into a stream to your right. After crossing a small bridge with a pond directly to your left, you'll parallel the pond shore to your left through the trees.

Turning right at the next intersection marks a definitive transition into deeper forest as you pass through a stone wall and up a hill through a mix of deciduous and hemlock. A large rock cliff will be to your left as you pass. You'll pass a wide-open meadow to your right, but continue now on the Wolf Pine Trail as you pass through mostly evergreen along with some large oak. Maintain your vigilance for possible deer sightings in this area. A ridge rises up from the forest floor to your left with some rock outcroppings visible as you progress.

Once you are on the Kettle Trail, you'll be traversing a flat forest floor surrounded by towering pine high up on a knoll. It is here that you have your best shot at spotting goshawks, which feed on birds like grouse and mammals such as chipmunks and squirrels. These hawks, identified by their long tail, short wings,

Pine grove on the edge of Appleton Meadows

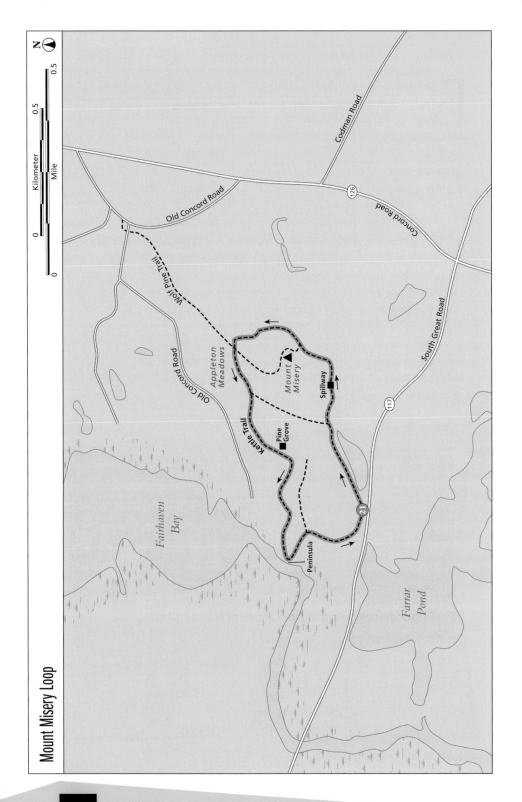

Mount Misery Loop

and white eye-stripe, are not as common as other species. As you begin descending, you'll see a pond down through the trees to your left. Now on an elevated trail bed within the forest floor, you'll have a steep embankment directly to your left populated with hemlock, and down to your right will be a marshy area that extends out to the Sudbury River in the distance. Even though approximately 15 miles have been designated as a Wild and Scenic River, development pressures and the accompanying high rate of water consumption continue to noticeably affect water flow during summer.

You'll reach the tip of a peninsula extending out toward the river surrounded by marsh on all sides. From here the trail heads back inland off this wooded peninsula. After topping a knoll within this grove, you'll see Route 117 down below in the distance. This is your cue that you are beginning to complete the loop. Your final descent to the parking lot is aided by log steps carved into the forest floor to prevent erosion.

MILES AND DIRECTIONS

0.0   Begin at trailhead through the split rail fence to the far right of the parking lot.

0.1   Pass a trail to your right, which cuts up some wooden stairs to Route 117.

0.2   Reach a spillway crossing made of stone emptying into a stream to your right.

0.3   Cross a small bridge with a pond directly to your left.

0.5   Reach another trail intersection marked by a large rock cliff to your left.

0.7   Pass straight through a four-way intersection, where you'll see access to a wide-open meadow to your right.

0.9   Reach another trail intersection where a small sign to your left marks the transition to the Kettle Trail.

1.0   Pass underneath a grand pine canopy high up on a knoll.

1.1   The trail bed is elevated here within the forest floor.

1.3   Reach the tip of a peninsula, which extends out toward the river surrounded by marsh on all sides.

1.5   Turn right at trail intersection, continuing to follow the Kettle Trail.

1.6   Descend log steps built into a hill; arrive back at the parking lot.

While this trail may not be surrounded by stately pine groves or possess historic intrigue, it's a lesser-traveled route that is more about getting away from it all with far fewer human encounters than the more publicized routes nearby. Why not make it a day and visit the DeCordova Museum at the trailhead? Outside in their thirty-five-acre outdoor sculpture park, you'll pass some spectacular life-size pieces. Inside, you'll be treated to a vast collection of contemporary works by local artists. Once you finally do get itchy feet, miles of undisturbed woods await circling Sandy Pond.

Start: Rear of the DeCordova Museum parking lot

Nearest town: Lincoln

Distance: 3.4-mile loop

Approximate hiking time: 2 hours

Difficulty: Easy

Trail surface: Packed earth, some pavement

Seasons: Year-round

Other trail users: Birders, snowshoers

Canine compatibility: Dogs allowed but prohibited from going in or near water (public water supply)

Land status: Town of Lincoln Conservation Department

Fees and permits: No charge

Schedule: Dawn to dusk daily

Maps: Available for purchase at www.lincolnconservation.org /LLCTBooksandMaps.html

Trail contacts: Lincoln Conservation Committee, Town Offices, Lincoln, MA 01773; (781) 259-2612; www.lincolntown.org

Finding the trailhead: Take exit 28B from Route 128 to Trapelo Road toward Lincoln. Follow Trapelo Road approximately 2.6 miles to a stop sign and intersection. Go straight through the intersection onto Sandy Pond Road. As soon as you begin passing the pond shore close by to your left, look to your left for a stone building and small parking lot. The lot's entrance is marked as 77 Sandy Pond with a yellow metal gate and a stone building overlooking the water. GPS: N42 25.7881 / W71 18.9607

THE HIKE

As you walk down Sandy Pond Road away from the parking lot and pass the intersection of Baker Bridge Road to your right, you'll pass older stately homes that appear to have once been summer retreats overlooking the pond shore. Once you turn left into the DeCordova Museum entrance and walk up a long driveway, you'll see some spectacular outdoor sculpture pieces up on the hill to your left and surrounding the driveway as you pass the metallic modernist ticket booth. Sculptures range from giant insects to larger-than-life shapes stacked on one another. Since you're walking, you won't have to pay a fee to pass through toward the far back of the museum parking lot. Even though the trailhead isn't marked with a signboard, there is a brown sign to the left posting rules of the trail and a blue sign with white lettering to the right identifying this area as a public water supply. You'll also see a small red triangle on a tree alongside the trail farther into the woods marking the way.

Elm, maple, and hickory surround the trail bed as you begin heading down a long hill with pond views off ahead through the trees. The trail bed continues to be wide open until you reach an old stone chimney complete with fireplace rising out of what used to be a cabin site to your right. Continuing past this landmark, the trail surface becomes more rugged as it traverses a hillside. You'll notice that trees

Sandy Pond is scenic even when iced-over in winter.

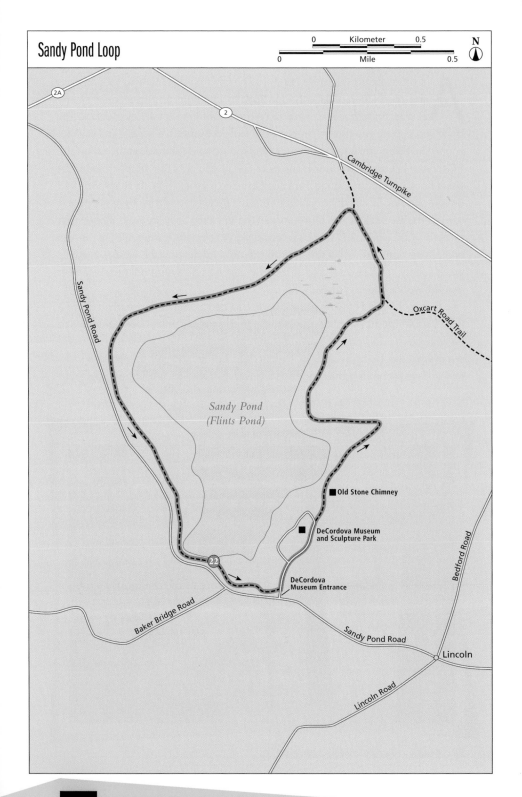

Sandy Pond Loop

Kilometer
0 0.5

Mile
0 0.5

N

2A

2

Cambridge Turnpike

Oxcart Road Trail

Sandy Pond Road

Sandy Pond
(Flints Pond)

■ Old Stone Chimney

■ DeCordova Museum
and Sculpture Park

22

DeCordova
Museum Entrance

Baker Bridge Road

Sandy Pond Road

Bedford Road

Lincoln

Lincoln Road

bordering the trail at different intervals are marked with red plastic circles. Shortly after cutting through a stone wall, you'll head down to the pond shore flanked with a marshy area visible through tree cover to your left.

You'll get increasingly clearer water views through the trees to your left as a stone wall parallels the trail through the trees to your right. Look carefully on your right for a small brown sign with white lettering pointing out where to continue at this potentially confusing intersection. This spot also marks a level plateau within the woods overlooking the water below through the trees. Once you turn left onto Oxcart Road Trail, a rough stone wall flanks each side of the trail surrounded by cherry, beech, and oak. Through the trees you'll see a house fairly close to the trail, and you'll hear road noise from Route 2 to your right.

You'll continue passing houses close by through the trees to your right with highly audible road traffic from Route 2. Cross a footbridge surrounded by underbrush along with larger swamp maple and oak. The presence of houses through the woods to your right continues although they are farther away than when you first started on the Oxcart Road Trail. You will soon make a permanent departure from any residential presence on this section of trail and begin to see the pond ahead in the distance through the trees.

The best view of Sandy Pond can be experienced upon passing through a stand of red pine, where to your left down through a wide-open field, you'll get a wide panoramic view of the entire pond. Descend a steep embankment within the woods and emerge into this same field skirting its far corner while paralleling Sandy Pond Road. Pass around a metal gate to your right and turn left onto Sandy Pond Road. You'll see the stone building in the distance where you parked on the opposite shore to your left. Follow the road back to the parking area.

MILES AND DIRECTIONS

0.0   Begin at a parking area next to a stone building on Sandy Pond near the intersection of Sandy Pond Road and Baker Bridge Road.

0.3   Turn left off Sandy Pond Road at the entrance to the DeCordova Museum to your left and walk up a long driveway.

0.5   Enjoy pond views ahead through the trees.

0.6   Reach an old stone chimney complete with fireplace rising out of what used to be a cabin site to your right.

0.7   Curve abruptly to the right, moving away from the pond shore.

0.8   Turn left at a T intersection onto the yellow-blazed trail.

1.1 Look carefully on the right for a small brown sign with white lettering pointing where to continue at this potentially confusing intersection.

1.3 Begin skirting a marshy area bordering the pond to your left.

1.4 Curve to the left at a trail split, passing a thick hemlock grove to your left.

1.5 Turn left at a small wooden signpost onto Oxcart Road trail.

1.7 Turn left at the 27 MILE marker.

1.8 Cross a footbridge surrounded by underbrush along with larger swamp maple and oak.

2.1 Depart close-up residential presence.

2.3 Transition away from wooded marsh surrounding the trail to mostly hemlock and small pine.

2.4 Turn sharply left, following yellow blazes.

2.6 Cross a small footbridge over a marshy area.

3.2 Enjoy a wide panoramic view of the entire pond down to your left through a wide-open field while passing through a red pine grove.

3.3 Turn left onto Sandy Pond Road.

3.4 Arrive back at the trailhead.

Wachusett Reservoir

This loop takes you through some massive pine groves and skirts the shores of the Wachusett Reservoir's equally expansive waters. Approximately 0.5 mile on this route has you hiking right at the water's edge for dramatic views and superb angling if you packed your fishing gear.

Start: Sawyer's Mills Gate #8 Trailhead

Nearest town: Boylston

Distance: 1.7-mile loop

Approximate hiking time: 1.5 hours

Difficulty: Easy

Trail surface: Packed earth, sand, and gravel

Seasons: Year-round

Other trail users: Birders, anglers, cross-country skiers, snowshoers

Canine compatibility: No dogs allowed

Land status: Massachusetts Department of Conservation and Recreation

Fees and permits: None

Schedule: Open one hour before sunrise to one hour before sunset year-round

Maps: Gate locations but not trail maps available at www.mass .gov/dcr/waterSupply/watershed /maps/WachusettResGates.pdf

Trail contacts: Department of Conservation and Recreation 251 Causeway Street, Suite 600, Boston, MA 02114-2104; (617) 626-1250

Other: Be sure not to miss the interpretive sign to the right side of the parking lot as you face the trailhead, which gives a detailed description and picture of the Sawyer's Mill site.

Finding the trailhead: From I-495 take exit 25 to I-290 west, then take exit 23 onto Route 140 north. Follow approximately 2 miles to the intersection of Route 70. Turn right onto Route 70 east and follow 3 miles to Gate #8 on your left. GPS: N42 22.4695 / W71 42.9452

Begin at the head of the parking lot behind a metal gate right off Route 70 up a short steep hill. A signboard will be to your right before making this climb on the right edge of the parking lot. You'll be ascending into a grand pine forest on a well-established wood road and quickly reach an unmarked three-way intersection. Continue straight on this perfectly level wood road surrounded by stately pine along with densely packed oak saplings and laurel on either side yet far back from the trail's edge. The forest canopy overhead is strikingly open and tall.

At the next three-way intersection, curve to the right through vast pine groves now populated by small to medium trees. After passing straight through a four-way intersection, the wood road gradually slopes downward, departing from large pine into mostly oak mixed with pine saplings. You'll get your first view of water straight ahead directly down through the trees to the waterfront. It's now apparent that you're heading out onto a point in the reservoir, and you'll reach its tip at about 0.7 mile; it's marked with a steel column poking out of the ground. Here you'll have some wide-open water views to either side before turning right and hugging the shore with this vast public water supply directly to your left and a steep and rugged wooded embankment largely punctuated with pine rising sharply to your right.

Wachusett Reservoir shoreline

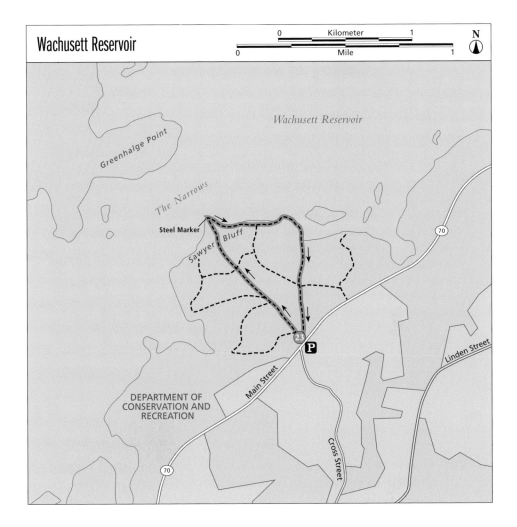

Wachusett Reservoir

This shoreline portion of the route skirts the edge of a cove with clear views of the opposite shore. You continue up close and personal with the waterfront until you turn right onto a wide, well-established wood road once again leading up through the pines and away from the water's edge. Soon cedars and oak enter the mix, and after a little climbing, the trail bed levels off temporarily through mostly evergreen before continuing on a gradual winding climb up to a wide four-way intersection. Now you'll be on a completely level and wide-open wood road surrounded by towering pines. Turn left when you return to the three-way intersection you first encountered on the route, and retrace your steps down through the metal gate to the parking lot.

23

Building the Wachusett Reservoir

As you walk along the shores of the Wachusett Reservoir, it's easy to imagine that this massive body of water has existed since the dawn of civilization, naturally carved by glaciers. Nothing, however, could be further from the truth. This reservoir is entirely man-made and was a massive undertaking that displaced multiple communities in its wake. Thousands of workers, many of them immigrants, were brought in to perform the manual labor. Don't forget, this was built between 1895 and1905, during the era of pickaxes and horses, long before steam shovels and power equipment became widely used. To accomplish this, 360 homes, 8 schools, 4 churches, 6 large mills, 19 miles of road, and more than 6 miles of railroad tracks were removed. Several cemeteries were even relocated to make way for this public water source that was so desperately needed to supply the growing city of Boston. One community displaced was the 200-resident village of Sawyers Mills, which was a thriving textile enterprise, with tenement houses for workers, a store, a post office, and railroad tracks. A detailed description of Sawyers Mills complete with a historic picture occupy a signboard to the right edge of the parking lot at Gate 8 as you face the trailhead.

MILES AND DIRECTIONS

0.0 Begin at trailhead leading from the head of the parking lot behind a metal gate right off Route 70 up a short steep hill. Continue straight through a three-way intersection.

0.3 Curve to the right through another three-way intersection continuing through vast pine groves now populated by small to medium trees.

0.5 Continue straight through a four-way intersection.

0.7 Reach a steel marker anchored in the ground on point in the reservoir.

1.2 Turn right, winding up and away from the waterfront on a wide wood road.

1.5 Continue straight through a wide four-way intersection.

1.7 After you pass through the original three-way intersection, arrive back at the trailhead.

Mount Pisgah Conservation Area

This loop provides a good overview of Mount Pisgah Conservation Area lands with virtually flat hiking except for the portion along the ridge leading up to Mount Pisgah. The clearest views are on the North View. It's often readily apparent that portions of this forest were harvested or cleared in the not-too-distant past.

Start: Smith Street Parking Lot
Nearest town: Northborough
Distance: 1.8-mile loop
Approximate hiking time: 1.5 hours
Difficulty: Easy
Trail surface: Packed earth with some rock
Seasons: Year-round
Other trail users: Birders
Canine compatibility: Dogs allowed under condition that owners clean up after
Land status: Town of Northborough Preservation Land
Fees and permits: None

Schedule: Open dawn to dusk year-round
Maps: Trail map board and pocket maps available at trailhead
Trail contacts: Sudbury Valley Trustees; 18 Wolbach Road, Sudbury, MA 01776; (978) 443-5588; svt@svtweb.org
Other: Fishers have been sighted in the woods surrounding the route. Hidden and rarely seen, these animals are fierce hunters who feed on rodents, small mammals like squirrels, and even porcupines, which they feast on by flipping them over onto their backs.

Finding the trailhead: From I-290 take exit 24. At the end of the ramp, turn onto Central Street toward the center of Boylston. After only about 100 feet, quickly turn right onto Ball Street and follow to its end. Turn left onto Green Street, and at 0.5 mile bear right at the fork onto Smith Road. Continue on Smith just over a quarter mile and turn right into the parking area. GPS: N42 21.5734 / W71 40.2628

Begin at the trailhead leading away from the parking lot and passing through a line of boulders. Walking straight ahead, you'll see a small white sign with black lettering indicating that you are now on the Mentzer Trail. You'll immediately enter a large pine grove on a flat trail surface passing by another trail sign to your right pointing to the Loop Trail. Continue straight since the Loop Trail is only a small loop and doesn't make an all-encompassing loop as the name might suggest. Small yellow circles sporadically affixed to trees bordering the trail mark this as the Yellow Trail. Once you cross seasonal Howard Brook over wood planks, you'll see on your left a small white sign with green lettering describing how this small stream is a key part of the forest ecosystem; for example, polliwogs are eaten by raccoons, which in turn are food for coyotes.

You will head back into dense pine groves until forking off to the right on the red-blazed Sparrow Trail. Here the trail noticeably skirts denser pine to your left, while to the right a younger, more deciduous mix becomes more prominent. The trail surface remains level, and shortly you'll pass another descriptive sign to your right indicating that you are passing through a stand of sugar maples. As soon as the trail makes a pronounced curve to the left, a stone wall parallels the trail close by to your right. Here you'll also begin making a slight climb through mostly

North View Overlook

young-growth black birch. Soon you'll pass through the stone wall that was paralleling the trail and notice that the surrounding trees are newer growth for as far as the eye can see. Since this noticeably flat area of the forest floor was clear-cut for box board wood in the days before cardboard, it is now remarkably wide open. Pass straight through the intersection with the Berlin Road Trail.

Once you turn left onto the Tyler Trail, you'll notice that red triangles now mark the trail. This will set you in the direction toward the North View, and here you'll notice that you're higher in elevation even though the grade is still relatively flat. Depending on the season, a lighter foliage cover will allow you to see the horizon through mostly young- to medium-growth oak, ash, and birch to your right. You'll now be steadily climbing at a gradual pitch on a ridge until you reach the Summit Connector Trail to your left. Continue straight on the red-blazed Tyler Trail until you intersect the yellow-blazed Mentzer Trail. Turn right, pass through a stone wall, and then walk along the trail bed flanked by a stone wall and large pine tree immediately to your left.

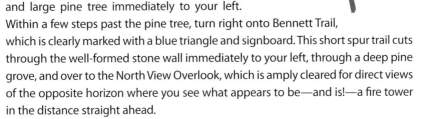

Within a few steps past the pine tree, turn right onto Bennett Trail, which is clearly marked with a blue triangle and signboard. This short spur trail cuts through the well-formed stone wall immediately to your left, through a deep pine grove, and over to the North View Overlook, which is amply cleared for direct views of the opposite horizon where you see what appears to be—and is!—a fire tower in the distance straight ahead.

Double back to the Mentzer Trail through mostly mid-growth oak on a level trail surface. Pass Tyler Trail on the left and proceed toward your second crossing of the Berlin Road Trail. Continue straight, following the yellow circles on the trees, and you'll sharply transition into a large pine grove. Emerging from this grove, complete the loop and retrace your steps on Sparrow Trail back to the parking lot.

Green Tip:
Carry a reusable water container that you fill at the tap. Bottled water is expensive, lots of petroleum is used to make the plastic bottles, and they're a disposal nightmare.

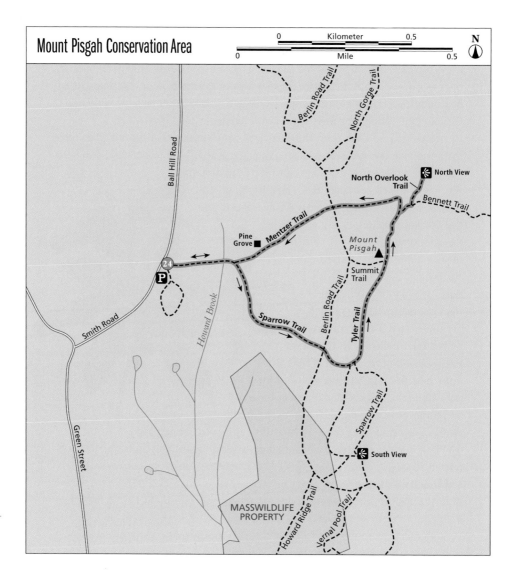

Mount Pisgah Conservation Area

0 Kilometer 0.5

0 Mile 0.5

N

Berlin Road Trail
North Gorge Trail
Ball Hill Road
North Overlook Trail
North View
Bennett Trail
Pine Grove
Mentzer Trail
Mount Pisgah
Summit Trail
Berlin Road Trail
Sparrow Trail
Tyler Trail
Smith Road
Howard Brook
24
P
Green Street
Sparrow Trail
South View
MASSWILDLIFE PROPERTY
Howard Ridge Trail
Vernal Pool Trail

MILES AND DIRECTIONS

0.0   Start at Mount Pisgah Trailhead.

0.1   Cross seasonal Howard Brook over a wood plank.

0.2   Fork off to the right onto the red-marked Sparrow Trail, skirting denser pine to your left.

0.4 Make a notable curve to your left while paralleling a stone wall close by to your right. Here you'll also begin making a slight climb through mostly young-growth black birch.

0.5 Cross the blue-blazed Berlin Road Trail.

0.6 As you turn left, continuing on the Tyler Trail, you'll notice red triangles marking the trail.

0.8 Continue straight past the Summit Connector Trail intersection to your left. You are now on the summit.

1.0 Turn right onto Bennett Trail, the yellow-blazed trail through a stone wall.

1.2 Enjoy the sights from the North View Overlook. Retrace your steps on the yellow-blazed Bennett Trail, returning to the loop. When you reach Tyler Trail, continue straight (west) on Mentzer Trail.

1.4 Cross the Berlin Road Trail, continuing on Mentzer.

1.5 Enter a large pine grove after being surrounded by mostly all deciduous trees.

1.6 Intersect with Sparrow Trail from the left; continue straight ahead toward the trailhead.

1.8 Arrive back at the parking lot.

Purgatory Chasm State Reservation

Perfect for a day of exploration, this unique 0.25-mile chasm runs between granite walls rising as high as 70 feet. Popular with picnickers and rock climbers alike, this formation was created with a sudden release of dammed-up glacial meltwater near the end of the last ice age, approximately 14,000 years ago. Trails lead to a wide variety of rock formations with names like The Corn Crib, The Coffin, The Pulpit, Lovers' Leap, and Fat Man's Misery.

Start: Across Purgatory Road from visitor center on a paved walkway
Nearest town: Whitinsville
Distance: 2.1-mile half cloverleaf
Approximate hiking time: 1.5 hours
Difficulty: Strenuous due to climbing rock ledge surrounding the chasm
Trail surface: Packed earth and rock
Seasons: Year-round
Other trail users: Rock climbers
Canine compatibility: Dogs must be leashed

Land status: Department of Conservation and Recreation
Fees and permits: None
Schedule: Sunrise to sunset daily
Maps: On signboard, in visitor center, and at www.mass.gov /dcr/parks/trails/print/Purgatory Chasm.pdf
Trail contacts: Department of Conservation and Recreation, Purgatory Chasm State Reservation Visitors Center, 198 Purgatory Road, Sutton, MA 01590; (508) 234-3733; www.mass.gov/dcr /parks/central/purg.htm

Finding the trailhead: From I-90, take exit 10A to Route 146 and follow Route 146 south to exit 6 in Sutton. Turn right onto Purgatory Road. Visitor center entrance and parking is 0.25 mile on your right. GPS: N42 7.7420/W71 42.8705

THE HIKE

Once you cross the street from the visitor center on Purgatory Road and curve away from the pavilion on top of the hill, you'll pass a curious stone round house with metal barred windows to your left. From here, you're surrounded by thick hemlock and a rocky forest floor as you traverse this level, well-graded footpath. You'll be able to catch glimpses of the chasm down through the trees to your right.

Once you reach the bottom of the hill, the trail levels off, and you're surrounded by younger-growth deciduous plants to your left with the mature pines that you passed through before now up to your right. You'll begin to hear a brook through the trees to your left and continue to hear it faintly when you begin climbing up toward the right side of the chasm on a wide, flat, sandy trail. You'll see a pine forest up on the cliffs to your left, and soon you'll be able to see the chasm up ahead. Follow the trail as it splits to the right over a rivulet while following blue markings as you begin scrambling up steep rock.

From this point forward while skirting the chasm to your left, you'll have plenty of opportunities to explore and climb, but exercise extreme caution. Rocks can be slick even with the slightest moisture, and in some cases you'll be on the edge of vertical drops. After doing some steady and steep climbing, you'll be rewarded where the footpath begins to level off high up above this ravine: There

Interesting building near the trailhead

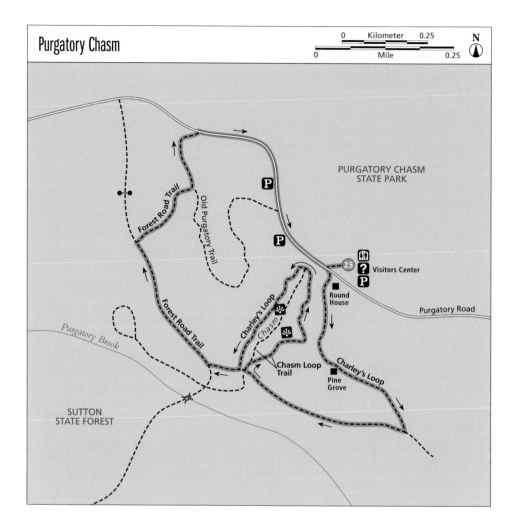

PURGATORY CHASM
STATE PARK

Forest Road Trail

Old Purgatory Trail

Forest Road Trail

Charley's Loop

Chasm

Purgatory Brook

Chasm Loop
Trail

Charley's Loop

Pine
Grove

25

Visitors Center

Round
House

Purgatory Road

SUTTON
STATE FOREST

are plenty of places to sit on the rocks and enjoy the views. After meandering along the rock cliffs, you'll begin to cut back down on the other side of the chasm, continuing to follow the yellow-blazed trail. You are now actually not that far from the trailhead where you began, but there is still more to explore. This side of the chasm is noticeably higher and more deeply wooded rather than up close to the edge for many portions.

As soon as you return to the intersection where you began climbing up into this chasm, turn right, following a sandy footpath, and shortly you'll intersect a wide dirt road. Turn right here, climbing steadily through almost all deciduous growth with pine in the mix to your right. You'll level off within the extensive pine forest surrounding you, and here it's clear that this section of the route is more remote and less heavily traveled since the main attraction is the chasm. Turn right off the dirt road to follow the blue blazes through pine and birch on a footpath, and you'll now be winding across the rocky forest floor surrounded by pine. Soon you'll be climbing up over these rocks until you reach a crucial T intersection, where you'll see spray-painted lettering on a tree in front of you pointing to PC (Purgatory Chasm) to the right and PR (Purgatory Road) to the left. Turn left and proceed back to Purgatory Road, and follow it back to the visitor center parking lot, completing the loop.

MILES AND DIRECTIONS

0.0 Cross Purgatory Road at a marked pedestrian crossing to the left of a map board that's in front of the visitor center onto a paved sidewalk.

0.3 Enter a pine grove, passing blue blazes on the trees to your left along with a stone marker.

0.4 Turn right at a T intersection onto a completely level trail surface.

0.6 Pass a blue trail spur to your right.

0.7 Turn right at a major intersection, heading up toward the chasm's right side on a wide, flat, sandy trail.

0.9 Enjoy views high above the chasm on rock ledges.

1.0 Begin cutting back down on the other side of the chasm, continuing to follow the yellow-blazed trail.

1.1 Climb over rock to your left on a short spur to an overlook of deep chasm views.

1.2 Curve toward the right, following a sandy footpath, and shortly you'll intersect a wide dirt road—Forest Road Trail—at the end of the loop.

1.4 Complete a steady climb on an access road within an extensive pine forest.

1.5 Turn right onto Forest Road Trail and follow the blue blazes through pine and birch on a footpath rather than an access road.

1.7 Turn left at a T intersection toward Purgatory Road.

1.9 Turn right onto Purgatory Road and follow it down the hill as it winds through large pine.

2.1 Reach the visitor center across the road to your left, completing the hike.

Blackstone River and Canal Heritage State Park

Featuring mostly flat walking except for the Goat Hill portion, this route takes you up close to remnants and faint imprints of the Blackstone Canal and River. There are plenty of bird-watching and fishing opportunities along the way as well.

Start: Brown metal gate at the head of the dirt parking lot
Nearest town: Northbridge
Distance: 4.8-mile out-and-back
Approximate hiking time: 2.5 hours
Difficulty: Moderate
Trail surface: Packed earth with some rock
Seasons: Year-round
Other trail users: Birders, anglers, snowshoers, mountain bikers
Canine compatibility: Dogs must be leashed

Land status: Department of Conservation and Recreation
Fees and permits: None
Schedule: 8:00 a.m. to sunset daily
Maps: On signboard at trailhead and at www.mass.gov/dcr/parks /images/blstMainMap.gif.
Trail contacts: Department of Conservation and Recreation, 251 Causeway Street, Suite 600, Boston, MA 02114-2104; (617) 626-1250

Finding the trailhead: From I-90, take exit 11 to Route 122 and follow Route 122 south 10.5 miles, passing through the towns of Grafton and Northbridge. After Northbridge at the next traffic light and major inter-section populated with fast food and retail, turn left onto Church Street. Parking lot marked with brown signage will be about 0.4 mile down to your right. GPS: N42 7.6741 / W71 38.3459

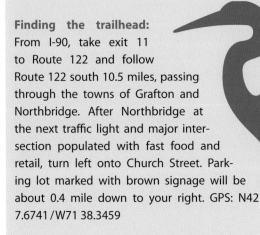

THE HIKE

Beginning at the trailhead, you'll notice the canal immediately to your left marked with a brown sign with white lettering affixed to a stone indicating that this is the Historic Blackstone Canal. Start off flat and straight on a wide, open grassy lane through this meadow, paralleling the canal to your left. Walking on what used to be the towpath, you'll soon be surrounded by some white pine and underbrush on either side.

Soon the pines thicken and become more numerous to your right. Depending on the season and weather conditions, portions of the trail can be muddy since the trail bed isn't lined with trap rock. You may have to negotiate soft spots and large puddles. A little less than 0.5 mile into the route, the canal is no longer a stagnant stretch of water but suddenly opens up into the Blackstone River.

The trail bed soon departs the towpath, and you'll be skirting the edge of an overgrown field to your right. The river will still be close by through the trees to your left, but it's a different ambience because you're walking on grass through a meadow interspersed with medium pine rather than traversing the towpath bed. After crossing a small wooden footbridge over a small, slow-moving stream, you'll again be up close to the river but now on a narrow footpath lined with copious tree roots.

Trail bed paralleling the Blackstone River

Although other footpaths intersect and veer off away from the river, follow this main trail, which most closely parallels the river. You'll reach a sharp curve in the trail marked with a post in the ground with a blue sign portraying a hiker symbol pointing to the right. As soon as you make this turn, the trail bed is now straight, flat, and elevated above a sandy wooded marsh on either side with the river in the distance to your left. Most of the trees now surrounding the trail are maple and ash, even though some pines remain in the mix.

The Blackstone Valley Canal

Inspired by the success of the Erie Canal in 1817 and necessitated by the proliferation of textile manufacturing along the Blackstone River in the early nineteenth century, the Blackstone Canal was built to link Central Massachusetts to the Atlantic Ocean. Between 1828 and 1848, horse-drawn boats carried freight and passengers between Worcester and Providence. This mode of transit proved to be highly efficient and successful until the railroad was completed in 1847, rendering the canal obsolete. Much evidence of the canal's initial infrastructure is lost to the ravages of time, but some lock chambers, dams, and bridges remain, serving as a reminder of the Blackstone Valley's rich industrial heritage and craftsmanship.

Canal stonework up close

As soon as you pass a large boulder to your left, you'll immediately begin to parallel what appears to be the old canal bed, which is now dried up, down an embankment to your right. As you're crossing a little wooden footbridge where the trail continues up into the woods, you'll see an immaculately preserved portion of the Blackstone Canal. Called Goat Hill Lock, the rock walls remain in remarkably good shape, providing the most definitive evidence on the route that the best engineering expertise and top-notch craftsmanship made the canal a success in its day.

After crossing this wooden footbridge from the modest pine grove on a point, you'll see a marsh through the trees to your left. Quickly passing this, you'll head up into the woods, climbing up onto a ridge surrounded by mostly oak, overlooking a vast marsh through the trees down to your left. Depending on the season, you'll get some clear, far-reaching views.

Once you hear Hartford Avenue up ahead through the trees, you'll turn to the right sharply up into the forest, departing from a footpath onto more of a rough access road carved into the side of a long hill with marsh views through the trees now to your right. Blue triangles mark this leg of the route as you climb higher with the surrounding forest floor carpeted with boulders. When the trail levels off, you'll reach an overlook up on a ridge with faraway marsh views. After descending Goat Hill and paralleling a moderately well-formed stone wall immediately to your left for a long stretch, you'll complete the loop within this route back to Goat Hill Lock. From here, retrace your steps back to the parking area.

MILES AND DIRECTIONS

0.0　Start to the left of a map board with a detailed description of the area, passing through a brown metal gate into an open field.

0.2　Pass a dirt road forking to your right, and continue straight alongside the canal, which is now noticeably narrower and grown in with underbrush.

0.4　To your left, the canal is no longer a stagnant stretch of water but suddenly opens up into the Blackstone River.

0.8　Depart the towpath, and the trail bed skirts the edge of an overgrown field to your right.

0.9　Cross a small wooden footbridge over a small, slow-moving stream.

1.0　Curve sharply to the right at a post in the ground with a blue sign portraying a hiker symbol.

1.4　Pass a large boulder to your left and immediately begin to parallel the old canal bed.

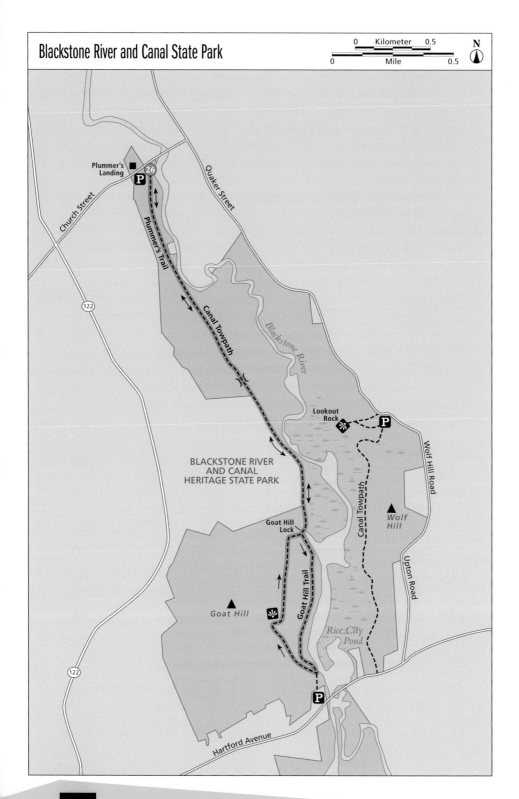

Blackstone River and Canal State Park

Plummer's Landing

26

Church Street

Quaker Street

Plummer's Trail

122

Canal Towpath

Blackstone River

Lookout Rock

Wolf Hill Road

BLACKSTONE RIVER
AND CANAL
HERITAGE STATE PARK

Canal Towpath

▲ *Wolf Hill*

Goat Hill Lock

Goat Hill Trail

Upton Road

▲ *Goat Hill*

Rice City Pond

122

Hartford Avenue

0   Kilometer   0.5

0   Mile   0.5

N

1.8 Turn right over a little wooden footbridge crossing Goat Hill Lock, an immaculately preserved portion of canal where the rock walls stand as monuments to fine craftsmanship.

1.9 Take the left fork to start the loop at a three-way intersection after climbing a small steep hill on a wood road.

2.3 Turn right sharply up into the forest, departing from a footpath onto more of a rough access road.

2.5 Turn to the right, reaching an overlook high up on a ridge. Continuing down a long hill within the forest, parallel a stone wall immediately to your left, extending down through the woods for a substantial distance ahead.

2.9 Reach the lock, and close the loop on Goat Mountain. Take the trail on the left alongside the river back toward the trailhead.

4.8 Arrive at the parking area.

🌱 Green Tip:
When you just have to go, dig a hole 6 to 8 inches deep and at least 200 feet from water, camps, and trails. Carry a ziplock bag to carry out toilet paper, or use a natural substitute such as leaves instead (but not poison ivy!!!). Fill in the hole with soil and other natural materials when you're done.

Rocky Narrows Preserve

Hike down the shores of the Charles River, starting at a canoe launch before climbing high within a short time up on a granite ridge above the narrows with 50-foot-tall rock walls on either side of the river. Nature watching abounds in the marshland fringing this river, which is not only a Boston landmark but also an important regional ecosystem.

Start: Begin from the parking lot through the meadow on a footpath to the left and away from the map board, which is straight ahead

Nearest town: Sherborn

Distance: 2.7-mile loop

Approximate hiking time: 1.5 hours

Difficulty: Easy

Trail surface: Packed earth, mowed grassland, and gravel

Seasons: Year-round

Other trail users: Birders, snowshoers, bikers, anglers, horseback riders, paddle boaters

Canine compatibility: Dogs allowed on leash

Land status: Trustees of Reservations property

Fees and permits: None

Schedule: Sunrise to sunset daily

Maps: Available online at www.thetrustees.org/assets/documents/places-to-visit/trailmaps/Rocky-Narrows-Trail-Map.pdf

Trail contacts: Trustees of Reservations, (978) 526-8687; seregion@ttor.org; www.thetrustees.org

Finding the trailhead: From the intersection of Routes 115 and 27, take Route 27 north for 0.4 mile and turn right onto Snow Street. At the next intersection, turn right onto Forest Street and follow it to a three-way intersection. You'll see the parking area to your right overlooking a rolling meadow down into the distance with a picnic table. The trailhead begins at the head of this meadow to the left of the signboard on a footpath through the grass. GPS: N42 13.57/W71 21.2384

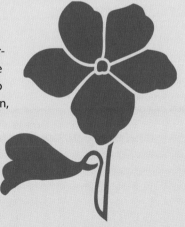

THE HIKE

Begin on the Red Trail by forking off to the left on a worn footpath sloping down through a wide-open meadow. After passing through a rough stone wall, turn right onto a sand and gravel access road now with woods immediately to your left while continuing to curve through meadow to your right. Heading straight down a footpath paralleling a stone wall to your right, you will first have underbrush on either side and then the forest floor quickly opens up with mature oaks. Much of the forest along this route was cleared for farming in the colonial era, but hardwoods and evergreens once again blanket the landscape.

After a stretch of level walking through patches of wooded marsh, you will pass through a hemlock and pine grove curving out to the Charles River shoreline where you'll be in a clearing used as a canoe landing. Retrace your steps back through the grove and now you are paralleling the Charles River though the trees to your left. If you keep noise to a minimum and tread softly, you may spot blue herons attracted to the river's surrounding marsh and standing water created by beaver dams.

Once you turn left at a small green sign with white lettering reading CAUTION: NARROW TRAIL STEEP LEDGE AHEAD, you'll immediately begin climbing steadily up a narrow footpath on more rugged and rocky terrain leading onto a ridge surrounded by thick hemlock. Down below to your left, you'll continue seeing marshlands

View of the Charles River from King Philip's Overlook

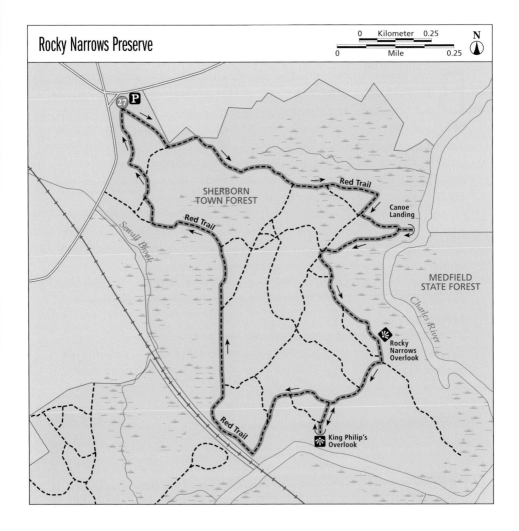

Kilometer 0.25
Mile 0.25
N

SHERBORN
TOWN FOREST

Red Trail

Red Trail

Canoe
Landing

MEDFIELD
STATE FOREST

Sewall Brook

Charles River

Rocky
Narrows
Overlook

Red Trail

King Philip's
Overlook

on either side of the Charles River as you're climbing along this ridge and reach Rocky Narrows Overlook, a clearing high above the ravine.

Farther along, a footpath to your left marked with a small pile of rocks leads to King Philip's Overlook. Once on this trail spur, you'll pass through wild blueberry and medium-size oak, crossing over some rock outcroppings into a grassy clearing. Continue toward a rock ledge precipice for wide, far-reaching views of the Charles River below. It was here that the 50-foot-high walls of granite on either side of the river were known as Gates of the Charles in colonial times. Both Wampanoag natives and Puritan colonists considered this river passage strategically important, especially during King Philip's War in 1675. Today these rocky cliffs are an excellent spot for watching hawks soar high above the river.

Retrace your steps back to the Red Trail and turn left, continuing on the main trail and steadily proceeding downward past narrower footpaths both to the left and right. Once you finally do turn right, you'll briefly see railroad tracks down a hill to your left. No sooner do you complete a steady climb through pine on a gravelly access road, you'll just as abruptly descend straight downward and then level out, all the while seeing the access road ahead far into the distance. At the bottom of the hill, you'll pass a red-blazed footpath to your left along with a wooded marsh; stay on the Red Trail. The trail bed is now surrounded by underbrush and then marsh continuing in the distance to your left.

Continuing straight and level, you'll pass a petroleum pipeline sign and then marsh down to your left. You'll finally curve up to the right into more stately pine, continuing on the more established footpath curving extremely close to somebody's house and backyard. After continuing level through more thick pine, you'll emerge back into the meadow with the signboard straight in front of you. Turn toward the left and head back to the parking lot, which is visible in the distance.

MILES AND DIRECTIONS

0.0 Fork to the left away from the signboard and picnic area down a worn footpath (the Red Trail) through wide-open meadow.

Meadow views from the Rocky Narrows trailhead

0.2 Continue straight at a fork in the trail down a footpath paralleling a stone wall to your right. Here you'll see a red marker and a small #22 sign on a tree to your right.

0.5 Fork to the left, continuing flat and following the red blazes.

0.7 Make a sharp right turn where you'll see a marsh directly ahead through the trees.

0.8 Make a sharp left turn, then pass through a hemlock and pine grove curving out to the Charles River, where you'll see a clearing used as a canoe landing. Continue clockwise on the Red Trail.

1.2 Reach a clearing—Rocky Narrows Overlook—that overlooks a ravine far below with some marsh and river views.

1.3 Continue straight through a four-way intersection, continuing on a slight incline surrounded by mostly oak.

1.5 Turn left onto a trail spur marked with a small pile of rocks leading to King Philip's Overlook. You'll pass through wild blueberry and medium-size oak, crossing over some rock outcroppings and into a grassy clearing. Continue toward a rock ledge precipice providing a good overlook of the river below. Return to the main trail and turn left.

1.7 Pass narrower footpaths both to the left and right as you steadily proceed downward on the main red-blazed trail.

1.8 Turn right, continuing on a gravelly access road but now steadily climbing through pine.

2.0 Pass a gravelly wood road to your right heading up into the woods.

2.3 Continue straight through another trail intersection with a marsh down below to your left.

2.4 Curve up to the right, continuing on the more established red-blazed footpath marked with a small white #9 sign with black lettering.

2.5 Continue following the red blazes by curving to the left close to the edge of a private property's backyard.

2.7 Return to the open meadow with signboard and turn left, returning to the parking lot.

Broadmoor Wildlife Sanctuary

An Audubon Society property, the Broadmoor Reservation lives up to its reputation as a birding sanctuary. As soon as you walk up to the Nature Center, meadows surround the pathway teeming with bluebird, wren, and other songbird activity encouraged by birdhouses and well-managed habitat. Farther along throughout this route you'll get up close to acres of marshland on an extensive series of boardwalks where you're sure to see the elusive wood duck or blue heron if you have binoculars.

Start: Proceed from the Audubon's Saltonstall Nature Center down a stone dust trail past a nature viewing platform to your left

Nearest town: Natick

Distance: 3-mile double loop

Approximate hiking time: 2 hours

Difficulty: Moderate

Trail surface: Packed earth, mowed grassland, and gravel

Seasons: Year-round

Other trail users: Birders

Canine compatibility: No dogs allowed

Land status: Massachusetts Audubon Society

Fees and permits: Fee for nonmembers

Schedule: 8:00 a.m. to 6:00 p.m. Tues–Sun and Mon holidays

Maps: Provided at visitor center with trail admission

Trail contacts: Massachusetts Audubon Society, 280 Elliot Street, Natick, MA 01760; (508) 655-2296; broadmoor@massaudubon.org

Finding the trailhead: Take exit 22 off I-95 and follow Route 16 west for 7 miles. The parking lot entrance will be to your left. Follow a sand and gravel driveway down to a crushed stone parking lot with a field and split rail fence to the right as you walk past the Saltonstall Nature Center to your left. GPS: N42 15.419 / W71 20.3613

After passing the Audubon's Saltonstall Nature Center, meadows behind a split rail fence on both sides of the trail and a bench to your left provide excellent opportunities for viewing songbirds like indigo buntings, mockingbirds, and bluebirds. Continue on crushed stone down a hill, where you'll quickly make a sharp curve to the left onto the accessible All Persons Trail. You'll see an extensive wooden boardwalk overlooking a marsh down ahead through the trees. Soon after turning right onto the Indian Brook Trail, you'll emerge along the lower edge of the field that borders the visitor center.

Continue along the mown grass trail bed through a larger meadow with a brushy woods line close to your right. Once you depart this meadow, you'll pass through some apple trees remaining from a long-ago farmstead where deer often feed. Once you transition to mostly swamp maple, the tree cover thickens and a boardwalk spur to your right leads to a small vernal pool. This is a perfect spot for viewing painted turtles or an occasional fox if you're fortunate and extra quiet. Soon after passing this planked walkway, you'll begin skirting Indian Brook Swamp to your left through the trees before climbing up on a slight incline above the swamp. The trail bed is surprisingly grassy for being in the middle of the woods.

Boardwalk section of trail overlooking marsh

Turn right onto Glacial Hill Trail. After passing through small to medium oak, swamp maple, and pine , turn left at a T intersection, where you'll quickly cross over a marsh on what appears to be a loosely constructed stone dam emerging into thick underbrush. At first it's confusing because there isn't an established trail bed in this spot, and it appears to dead-end at a hill straight ahead. However, your persistence in curving through the brush to your right will put you back on a worn footpath with the marsh close by to your right and steep Glacial Hill rising abruptly to your left.

Turn right once you reach a T intersection, where you'll see erosion bars built into the forest floor rising up into hills in both directions. You'll now be on a narrow footpath loop encircling kettle ponds within a "bowl" on Glacial Hill. The trail descends down from the ridge, passing the waters' edge close by to your left. After passing a second kettle pond, you'll gradually climb out of this bowl back onto the ridge. You'll level off high up on a knoll surrounded by blueberry bushes and medium oak, where you can enjoy some expansive marsh views.

Broadmoor's Nature Center Is Green

No, I'm not talking about the building's color. As you pass the Broadmoor Reservation's Saltonstall Nature Center to your left at the trailhead, you'll see display boards attached to the wall explaining the building's solar system, which is highly visible for all to see.

An antique horse barn built in 1911, the Nature Center was renovated in 1983 to incorporate a variety of environment-friendly materials and renewable energy resources, which now reduce energy consumption by 80 percent.

The ceiling and walls are lined with superinsulated plastic sheets, providing a draft-proof vapor barrier. Solar provides most of the winter heating needs supplemented with a woodstove, which only uses about one and a half cords of wood each year. Large picture windows also attract natural sunlight, and photovoltaic panels installed on the roof convert the sunlight into electricity, meeting 100 percent of the center's power consumption.

Indoor composting toilets have saved over 2.2 million gallons of water over the past twenty years along with a Smart Storm system, which collects and stores 1,200 gallons of rainwater per year from the building's roof. This is then used for watering landscape plantings surrounding the sanctuary.

You can check out the building's latest solar energy data, such as amount generated per day, along with pollution and energy equivalents at www .sunviewer.net/portals/MassAudubon/.

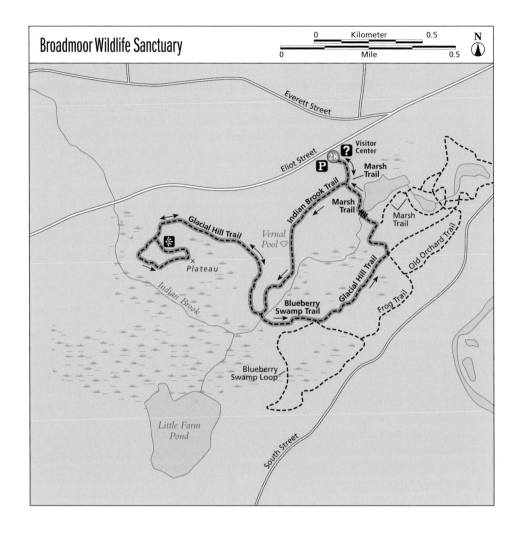

After retracing your steps back down the Glacial Hill Trail where it intersects the Indian Brook Trail once again, continue straight this time, onto the Blueberry Swamp Trail. You'll cross Indian Brook over a small wooden bridge flanked by marsh on either side. Take your time because chances are you'll spot painted turtles sunning themselves out on a log or see some wood ducks, great blue herons, or kingfishers. After crossing this brook, you'll head into a pine grove onto a better established wood road. From here, the route continues level on an open forest floor surrounded by large pine and low-growing wild blueberry bushes with Indian Brook Swamp particularly visible through the trees to your left.

Still under the cover of thick pine, you'll pass a bench to your left off the trail overlooking the water's edge. Turn left (north) onto the Marsh Trail. After crossing two more elaborate wooden boardwalks over marsh, you'll complete the loop once you cross a small wooden bridge. From here turn right, retracing your steps back up to the visitor center and parking area.

MILES AND DIRECTIONS

0.0 Pass a nature viewing platform to your left and a wide-open meadow behind a split rail fence to your right.

0.1 Turn sharply right, continuing on stone dust several paces to another trail intersection, and turn right onto the Indian Brook Trail, marked with a small sign.

0.3 Depart the meadow, passing through some apple trees remaining from long-ago farm usage.

0.5 Depart from marsh views to your left, veering into a more wooded interior.

0.7 Turn right at a T intersection onto the Glacial Hill Trail.

1.1 Turn left at a T intersection, heading down toward a marsh, which you'll soon be crossing.

1.2 Turn right at the Glacial Hill Trail Loop marker.

1.4 Level off on a plateau surrounded by blueberry bushes high up on a knoll.

1.5 Reach the highest elevation you'll be at along this route with marsh views down through the trees and into the distance.

1.9 Continue straight ahead at the three-way intersection, rejoining the main loop

2.1 Turn left at a four-way intersection, continuing on the Blueberry Swamp Trail.

2.3 Emerge into a meadow and turn left at a four-way intersection onto the Marsh Trail.

2.7 Stay to the left, continuing on the Marsh Trail and passing onto a wooden boardwalk.

2.9 Pass the entrance to an extensive boardwalk (All Persons Trail) to your right and within a few steps complete the loop.

3.0 Arrive back at the trailhead.

Noanet Woodlands

This 800-acre preserve offers a good mix of passive recreation like fishing in the mill pond for blue gills, summit views of the Boston skyline, and an historic ironwork site. This is all possible due not only to the foresight of Amelia Peabody, who added to her estate over the years, but also to her generosity in donating it for public use while she was still alive.

Start: To the left-hand side of the parking lot as you're pulling in with the tennis courts to your right. Begin at the map board with giveaway trail maps.
Nearest town: Dover
Distance: 2.6-mile lollipop
Approximate hiking time: 1.5 hours
Difficulty: Moderate
Trail surface: Packed earth, rock, and gravel
Seasons: Year-round
Other trail users: Birders, snowshoers, anglers, mountain bikers, horseback riders

Canine compatibility: Dogs allowed on trail but not in Caryl Park
Land status: Trustees of Reservations property
Fees and permits: None
Schedule: Sunrise to sunset daily
Maps: Available at trailhead and online at www.thetrustees.org /assets/documents/places-to -visit/trailmaps/NW_Web_TMap _Jan2010.pdf
Trail contacts: Trustees of Reservations, (508) 785-0339; seregion @ttor.org; www.thetrustees.org

Finding the trailhead: From I-95, take exit 17 onto Route 135, aka West Street. Continue 0.6 mile, turning left onto South Street. After 1.8 miles, South Street becomes Willow Street. Turn right onto Dedham Street, continuing 0.3 mile to Caryl Park. The parking lot entrance is easy to miss since it's hidden to the left-hand side of the tennis courts in Caryl Park. A white barn with green window trim to your left is a signal that the entrance is a little farther up as you continue on Dedham Street. GPS: N42 14.8525/W71 16.1462

THE HIKE

Although it's difficult to spot the trailhead parking area from Dedham Street, once you're in the parking lot alongside the tennis courts in Caryl Park, signs leave you with no doubt as to where to begin hiking.

You'll pass between a small wooden outbuilding painted white to your left and a map board with giveaway maps to your right with a sign welcoming you to the Noanet Woodlands Reservation. Traversing a footpath through pine, you'll quickly reach a dirt access road where you want to turn right. As you progress, you'll see a yellow circle up on a tree marking the route. Following these yellow circles, you'll shortly fork off to the left back into the woods on a footpath. You'll also see a sign up on a tree at this fork stating You are in Caryl Park, Welcome to Noanet Woodlands.

You'll soon cross over a small stream running through a drainage pipe on an established wood road. Marshy woods will be to your left as you continue level curving up on a main path away from a footpath to left. Turn left upon reaching a key intersection marked with a sign indicating that you're leaving Caryl Park, another welcoming you to Noanet Woodlands, along with blue and red markings on a tree. Just steps ahead up an incline, turn right at the #4 marker, following the blue blazes. After passing under red pine, you'll reach a grassy clearing with a series of telephone poles stacked three tall lengthwise at different intervals. These hurdles are installed for the enjoyment of horseback riders.

Noanet Peak overlook

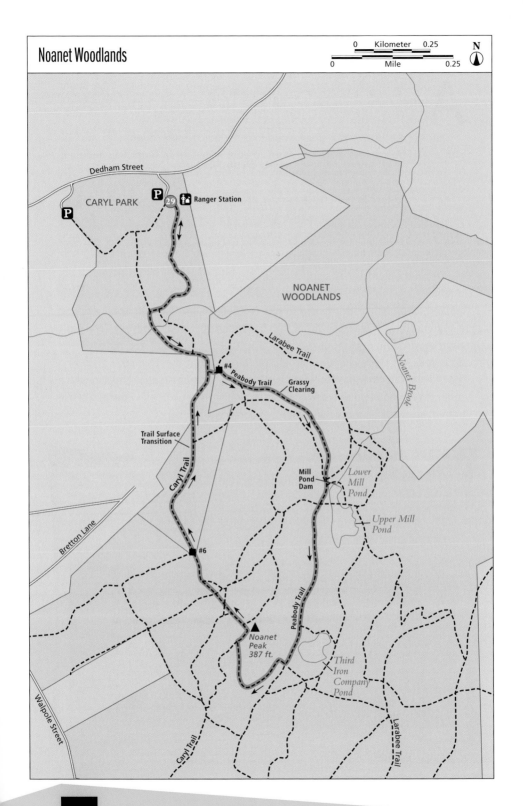

Noanet Woodlands

0　Kilometer　0.25
0　Mile　0.25

N

Dedham Street

CARYL PARK

P

P

29 Ranger Station

NOANET
WOODLANDS

Noanet Brook

Larabee Trail

#4

Peabody Trail

Grassy
Clearing

Trail Surface
Transition

Caryl Trail

Mill
Pond
Dam

*Lower
Mill
Pond*

*Upper Mill
Pond*

Bretton Lane

#6

Peabody Trail

Noanet
Peak
387 ft.

*Third
Iron
Company
Pond*

Walpole Street

Caryl Trail

Larabee Trail

Continue by forking to the left onto a level, well-graded carriage road. The roadbed is carved into a hillside with a steep bank directly to your right and steep hill down to your left. After steadily descending through pine, turn left onto a trail spur leading down to a stone dam and spillway from a mill pond above cascading onto rocks below. This is all that remains of a nineteenth-century iron works that attempted to harness the Noanet Brook's water flow.

When you're done exploring, turn left, continuing on the blue-blazed Peabody Trail, and soon you'll be curving away from the mill pond as you reach a clearing with a fork in the trail. Although you'll see a sign to your right pointing to Noanet Peak, continue flat and straight on the Peabody Trail. At your next four-way intersection, turn right onto a steep, unmarked footpath leading to Noanet Peak. You'll scale some steep rock ledge, and as soon as you reach the top, turn right over to an outcropping with blue sky visible in the distance. You are now on 387-foot-tall Noanet Peak, where you'll have Boston skyline views and hawk watching during the fall.

Noanet Millpond Spillway

Retrace your steps from here and then turn right at a post straight ahead, passing through a wide, grassy intersection pocked with stones. The trail descends sharply down a long hill over wood chips. You'll pass narrower, less-traveled footpaths to your left and right, but continue straight down on this wide trail bed. As soon as the trail levels out, you'll be surrounded by large pine and then pass over a rock wash surrounded by wild blueberry bushes. A little past the Caryl Trail intersection, you'll pass a cluster of three medium beech trees with carved bark to your left. Since there aren't any others in the vicinity, they stick out prominently. You'll skirt the edge of somebody's backyard once the trail surface changes to stone dust and then another house through the trees to your left. Continue straight through the next trail intersection, where you'll now be retracing your steps back to the parking area.

MILES AND DIRECTIONS

0.0 Pass between a small wooden outbuilding painted white to your left and a map board with giveaway maps to your right.

0.3 Turn left at a T intersection onto an established wood road, quickly crossing over a small stream running through a drainage pipe across the trail.

0.5 Turn left at a key intersection marked with a sign indicating that you're leaving Caryl Park and another welcoming you to Noanet Woodlands.

0.7 Reach a grassy clearing and bear left on a level, well-graded carriage road.

0.9 Turn left onto a trail spur leading down to a stone dam and spillway.

1.3 Catch glimpses of Third Iron Company pond to your left through the trees.

1.4 Turn right at a four-way intersection onto a steep, unmarked footpath leading to Noanet Peak.

1.6 Enjoy views from the peak.

1.7 Cross the Caryl Trail where you'll see a #6 marker on a tree.

1.9 Transition from dirt to a mixture of crushed stone and stone dust trail surface.

2.6 Return to the parking lot after completing the loop and retracing your steps.

Wilson Mountain Reservation

Rise quickly through thick pine groves high up onto a ridge with Boston skyline views. This route has some challenging rock scrambles leading to the overlook, but a high percentage of the trail surface is level and wide.

Start: From the small paved parking lot, pass around a green metal gate onto a gravel access road

Nearest town: Dedham

Distance: 1.6-mile loop

Approximate hiking time: 1.5 hours

Difficulty: Moderate

Trail surface: Packed earth, rock, and gravel

Seasons: Year-round

Other trail users: Birders

Canine compatibility: Dogs allowed on leash

Land status: Massachusetts Department of Conservation and Recreation

Fees and permits: None

Schedule: Sunrise to sunset daily

Maps: Available at www.topo.com

Trail contacts: Department of Conservation and Recreation, 251 Causeway Street, Suite 600, Boston, MA 02114-2104; (617) 626-1250

Finding the trailhead: From Route 128, take exit 17 onto Route 135 east. After approximately 0.7 mile, park at the second small lot to your left, which is paved and overlooks a ballfield. GPS: N42 15.5423 / W71 11.8506

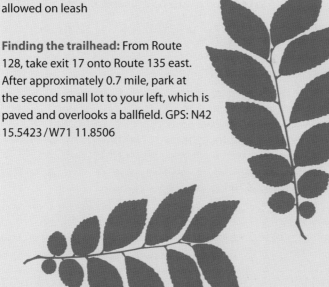

You'll quickly pass a blue-blazed trail to your right near the trailhead, but continue straight on a level, red-blazed access road through a mixed forest of pine and deciduous growth. Turn right upon reaching a split in the trail, passing into a thick pine grove now gradually climbing on a trail bed blanketed with pine needles. The trail gets more rugged as you wind up through rock outcroppings. If local residents hadn't joined forces and petitioned the Commonwealth of Massachusetts to preserve this ridgeline as open space back in 1994, the forest would now be suburban tract housing.

You'll pass a boulder tumble up to your left as you continue on what has become a narrow footpath within this shaded portion of forest. Climbing farther, the forest canopy opens up, allowing more sunlight to shine through, and as you

Climbing up Wilson Mountain

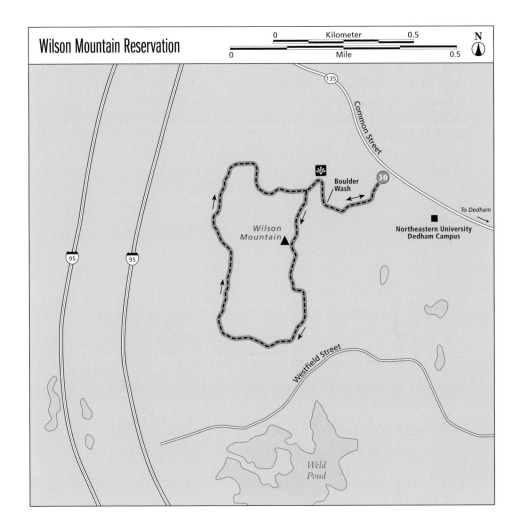

level out, the surrounding forest is a 50/50 mix of deciduous trees and pine. After scrambling up an extensive rock outcropping, you'll reach a grassy overlook of the Boston skyline marked with a large glacial erratic. Climb up on top of this boulder for more of a bird's-eye view.

Continue on a level trail bed, passing more rock formations poking out of the forest floor particularly to your left. You're at a noticeably higher elevation on the forest floor progressing along a ridge, but soon you'll wind downhill onto a plateau within the woods. The trail surface is wide and rocky in some places, heading through mostly hemlock and pine on a ridge. Be aware of roots on the trail bed since there are many in this section.

Soon you'll pass through a hemlock grove with laurel clustered directly to your left and a wide-open forest floor to your right. After curving to the right at the next trail intersection, following the blue blazes, you'll begin crossing a series of small wooden footbridges first over a tiny stream and then a marshy area surrounded by mostly pine and newer-growth deciduous plants. You'll climb back up onto a ridge after crossing a relatively large marsh, level out, and then as the trail widens descend gradually but for a long stretch surrounded by wild blueberries, oak, beech, and black birch.

Once you cross a brook and turn right at the next T intersection, you are now on the mountain's northern face. Since it is shielded from the more intense summer rays of sun, white and yellow birch groves thrive here. Continuing on this trail connects you back to the Boston skyline overlook. Retrace your steps from here back down to the parking area.

MILES AND DIRECTIONS

0.0   Begin on a level gravel access road through a mixed forest of pine and deciduous trees.

0.1   Turn right at a split in the trail into a thick pine grove.

0.2   Pass a tumble of boulders up to your left.

0.25   After traversing an extensive rock outcropping, reach an overlook with clear Boston skyline views.

0.3   Turn left at a T intersection to walk the loop clockwise.

0.4   Turn left onto a blue-blazed trail.

0.7   Continue by curving to the right at a trail intersection following the blue blazes.

1.2   Turn right at a T intersection after a brook crosses underneath the trail.

1.3   Complete the loop and continue straight toward the trailhead.

1.6   Retrace your steps upon returning to the Boston skyline overlook back down to the parking area.

Rocky Woods Reservation

If you've brought the family along for this route, you're in luck! This reservation not only has deep woods hiking but also ponds with easy access points, picnic areas, a volleyball court, horseshoe pits, and a spacious pavilion just in case the weather isn't cooperating.

Start: Behind the gatehouse at map board on the Loop Trail
Nearest town: Medfield
Distance: 3-mile loop
Approximate hiking time: 1.5 hours
Difficulty: Moderate
Trail surface: Packed earth, rock, and gravel
Seasons: Year-round
Other trail users: Birders, snowshoers, horseback riders, anglers
Canine compatibility: Dog walking by permit only, subject to restrictions

Land status: Trustees of Reservations property
Fees and permits: Fee for nonmembers
Schedule: Sunrise to sunset daily
Maps: Available at the trailhead and at www.thetrustees.org /assets/documents/places-to -visit/trailmaps/Rocky-Woods -Fork-Factory-Brook-Trail-Map.pdf
Trail contacts: Trustees of Reservations, (978) 526-8687; neregion @ttor.org; www.thetrustees.org

Finding the trailhead: From I-95, take exit 16B onto Route 109 West and follow for 5.7 miles. Turn sharply right onto Hartford Street, following 3.1 miles to entrance on right. GPS: N42 12.359 / W71 16.6095

Walk back down through the large sand and gravel parking lot and pass behind the gatehouse, reaching a map signboard at the trailhead. Begin on a wide footpath paralleling Hartford Street to your left before turning right, passing behind two metal posts spanned with chain. You'll now be on a level access road passing through mostly large to medium oak and soon see a brown sign with white lettering indicating this is the Loop Trail.

You'll soon pass over a narrow brook flanked with small magnolia and swamp maple on either side. From here the trail carves into a hillside as you are steadily climbing through the woods where you'll get your first views of Echo Pond through the underbrush to your right. Soon you'll see a wooden boardwalk to your right crossing Echo Pond. This is a great opportunity to head out here for some pond views and, if you brought your pole, some catch-and-release fishing. Just remember that to continue this route, don't cross to the other shore. Double back, continuing to follow the Echo Pond Trail with the pond shore close by to your right.

Soon you'll climb away from the pond up a hill on a dirt and stone footpath, passing through red pine with small magnolia and wild blueberry bushes border-

Trail bed along the Ridge Trail

ing the trail. As the trail levels off, you'll be winding through the forest past sporadic boulders in the woods on either side, especially to your right. Wooded swamp meets the trail edge at one point before you turn right onto the East and West Trail. This level gravel access road continues onto the June Pond Trail, where you'll immediately be traveling through thick small pines crowding in on either side of the trail. You'll get your first glimpses of marshy June Pond down through the trees to your right as you're up on an elevated trail bed. This portion was clearly built up above the pond because to your left the forest floor naturally meets the trail's edge.

Immediately upon turning onto the Ridge Trail, you'll be surrounded by rugged rocky terrain and mostly pine as you visibly move up and away from the pond. You'll see that the trail name is apropos as you're climbing steadily up onto a rocky ridge with large boulders on either side dropped by glacial action years ago. As soon as you begin passing through low-growing wild blueberry bushes on either side, the trail has leveled off completely. Soon the trail bed transitions from being a wide footpath to a gravel access road. You'll pass a short trail spur to your right leading to a seasonal overlook on a rock ridge. If you're passing through when leaves are on the trees, it's not worth exploring.

After this overlook, the trail steadily descends, eventually leveling off in a clearing with a confluence of trails. Here you'll see Chickering Pond to your right through the trees before turning left onto the Tower Trail spur. Begin a steep and steady climb on a wide trap-rock access road with thick pine to your right. Erosion bars with shredded shingles in between them will soon be built into the steep and winding trail surface. Following a small sign on a tree pointing to VISTA, you'll now be progressing on relatively level ground and reach a clearing up on a ridge with concrete anchors where a radio tower once stood. You are clearly on top of Cedar Hill although trees block any views and the trail transitions to a narrow footpath over rock. You'll be climbing slightly downward toward a rock ledge, which serves as the clearest overlook available on this hill. Pay particular attention to a narrow footpath passing away from this clearing down through rock and wild blueberries. After enjoying horizon views, take this trail connecting back down to Tower Trail and the shores of Chickering Pond, where you'll pass a level clearing on the water perfect for fishing or launching a canoe. Sunfish and bass are plentiful here during spring and summer, but don't forget that it's catch-and-release only.

The access road from now until the end of this route is flat and wide, leading through the recreational portion of this reservation. Soon the path will open up into a clearing to your right with picnic tables overlooking the pond. Curving to the right, the trail surface transitions from stone dust to pavement, and you'll see a volleyball court and pavilion to your right. Continue on the pavement until you complete the loop back at the parking lot.

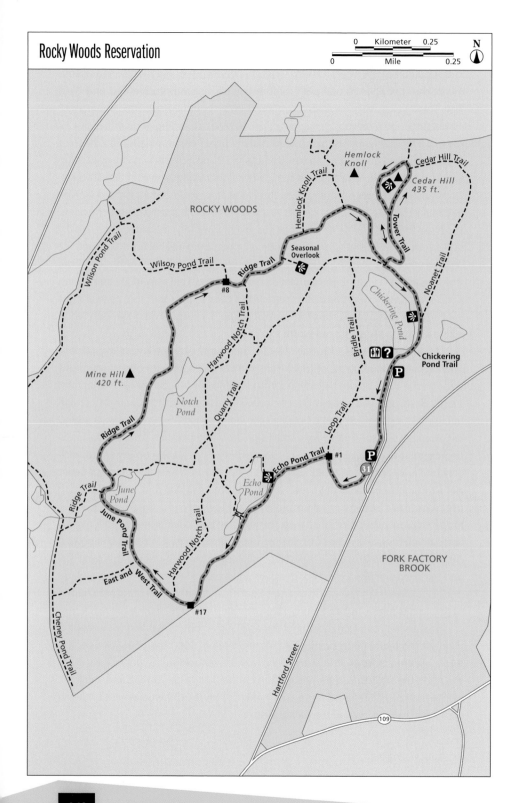

Rocky Woods Reservation

0 — Kilometer — 0.25
0 — Mile — 0.25

N

ROCKY WOODS

Hemlock Knoll ▲

Cedar Hill Trail

Cedar Hill 435 ft. ▲

Hemlock Knoll Trail

Tower Trail

Seasonal Overlook

Wilson Pond Trail

Ridge Trail

#8

Chickering Pond

Noanet Trail

Harwood Notch Trail

Bridle Trail

Chickering Pond Trail

P

Mine Hill 420 ft. ▲

Notch Pond

Quarry Trail

Loop Trail

Ridge Trail

P

31

June Pond

Echo Pond

Echo Pond Trail

#1

Ridge Trail

June Pond Trail

Harwood Notch Trail

FORK FACTORY BROOK

East and West Trail

#17

Cheney Pond Trail

Hartford Street

109

Catch-and-Release Fishing

Chickering and Echo Ponds, originally built as fire suppression pump ponds, are now premier attractions at Rocky Woods Preserve, providing swimming and excellent fishing opportunities. Before casting your line and trying your luck, keep in mind that catch-and-release fishing is the best approach toward ensuring a promising future for this sport.

Freshwater fish face decreasing habitat along with ever-increasing numbers of anglers. Even with the best intentions and following the adage of "a fish is too valuable to catch only once," it's inevitable that some fish you release will die anyway. Here are some tips for increasing their odds of survival.

Use artificial lures: Fish rarely survive being hooked with bait since they tend to swallow the hook. Artificial lures and flies, which fish tend to bite but not swallow, are hooked in the mouth, making them easier and less damaging to extract.

Use a cotton mesh net: Nets with a hard plastic mesh usually scrape the fish, removing its protective mucous coating. Remember to have half the net in the water and then lead the fish into it headfirst.

Release gently: Never throw a fish back into the water or release it into a strong current. Instead, slide the fish into calmer waters with its head facing the current.

Chickering Pond shore

MILES AND DIRECTIONS

0.0 Walk back down through the large sand and gravel parking lot, passing behind the gatehouse, where you'll see a map signboard at the trailhead.

0.1 Fork to the left at a T intersection marked with a small #1 sign up on a tree onto the Echo Pond Trail.

0.2 Catch your first views of Echo Pond through the underbrush to your right.

0.5 Turn right onto the East and West Trail, a level gravel access road marked with a small #17 sign.

0.7 Turn right onto the June Pond Trail.

0.9 Turn right at a T intersection, continuing with the pond shore close up to your right.

1.0 Fork to the left within a matter of steps at another intersection, continuing on the Ridge Trail.

1.5 Turn right at a T intersection with a #8 marker sign up on a tree, and literally five steps farther you'll pass the Harwood Notch Trail to your right, but continue on the Ridge Trail by forking to the left.

1.6 Pass a short trail spur to your right to a seasonal overlook on a rock ridge.

2.0 Turn left onto the Tower Trail spur after passing through a wide confluence of trails.

2.3 Turn left at a T intersection, following a small sign on a tree pointing to VISTA.

2.5 Turn right heading back down the Ridge Trail

2.7 Turn left upon reaching the #3-marked T intersection heading toward the pond shore to your right.

3.0 Arrive back at the trailhead.

Noon Hill Reservation

Although you wouldn't know it based on the remote location, this reservation is situated in historic Medfield. Noon Hill and the surrounding rock ledge are the result of glacial action that carved depressions in the earth's surface thousands of years ago. Today, the surrounding landscape encompasses marsh and higher-elevation forest within minutes all on the same route.

Start: Behind a green metal gate above the parking lot on a wide, level trail

Nearest town: Medfield

Distance: 1.7-mile loop

Approximate hiking time: 1.5 hours

Difficulty: Moderate

Trail surface: Packed earth, rock, sand, and gravel

Seasons: Year-round

Other trail users: Birders, snowshoers, bikers, anglers

Canine compatibility: Dogs allowed

Land status: Trustees of Reservations property

Fees and permits: None

Schedule: Sunrise to sunset daily

Maps: Available at the trailhead and online at www.thetrustees .org/assets/documents/places-to -visit/trailmaps/NH_Web_TMap _Jan2010.pdf

Trail contacts: Trustees of Reservations, (978) 526-8687; seregion@ttor.org; www.thetrust ees.org

Finding the trailhead: From the intersection of Routes 27 and 109 in Medfield, follow Route 109 west for 0.1 mile. Immediately turn left onto Causeway Street and follow 1.3 miles. Turn left onto Noon Hill Road. Parking lot large enough for 15 cars will be on your right. GPS: N42 9.8857 / W71 19.0869

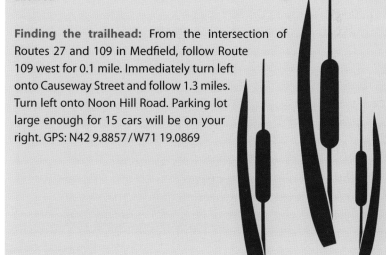

After walking past a map board with giveaway maps to your right, pass around a green metal gate onto a wide trail that's flat and straight through a mix of oak and pine. Up ahead to your right, you'll pass a sign that welcomes you to the Bay Circuit Trail and also provides a description and map of its route as it encircles the entire Massachusetts Bay. You'll be passing through a mix of deciduous trees with some grand pines in the mix. Since the habitat is favorable for ruffed grouse, you are likely to be startled by the sudden burst of this bird's fluttering wings if you approach one along the trail.

Continue straight on this well-established wood road with a stone wall now paralleling the trail bed to your left. As you progress from being surrounded by pine to exclusively beech and swamp maple, you'll notice that the trail bed can be muddy in spots depending on the season and precipitation. After completing a long and steady climb, you'll level off, passing through a mix of pine and deciduous growth at a higher elevation before gradually heading down a slope. As soon as you reach a little white sign with black lettering indicating the number 6 to your right, turn left onto a wood road that is easy to miss. You'll be gradually climbing once more now, passing through rugged terrain punctuated with rock outcroppings on either side.

Overlook

Once you reach a wide, grassy trail intersection, turn right onto a trail spur leading up to Noon Hill. You'll be traversing rock ledge in spots, passing a thick pine grove to your left, and then quickly emerging on top of a rock cliff outfitted with a stone bench overlooking the valley below with some good horizon views. As legend has it, it's here that early settlers noticed that the sun rose above this hill at noontime. During autumn, this is the place to be for watching hawks as they migrate south for the winter.

Once you're back on the main trail, you'll be traversing a rocky ridge within the forest floor, gradually climbing higher in elevation. Soon you'll curve off this ridge, winding down through a rocky forest floor on a trail marked with blue diamond or square blazes. Heading down through mostly oak and beech, you'll soon parallel a stone wall to your left and see that several rock sculptures have been created by other creative hikers piling smaller stones from the wall in various patterns. This trail segment is noticeably newer since it's narrower and less worn than the rest of the route as it winds up and down small ridges within the woods. Once you dead-end at a T intersection, you've completed the loop. Turn right here and retrace your steps back to the parking area.

MILES AND DIRECTIONS

0.0 Walk around a green metal gate onto a wide trail that's flat and straight through a mix of oak and pine.

0.3 Continue straight past a trail forking off to your left marked with a boulder alongside. You'll return on this trail when you complete the loop portion of the hike.

0.5 Begin a long and steady climb up from beech and swamp maple into a mix of pine and deciduous growth at a higher elevation.

0.7 Turn left at a little white sign with a black #6 to your right onto a wood road.

0.9 Turn right onto a trail spur at a wide grassy trail intersection leading up to Noon Hill overlook.

1.2 Turn left at the T intersection marked #8A on a small white sign.

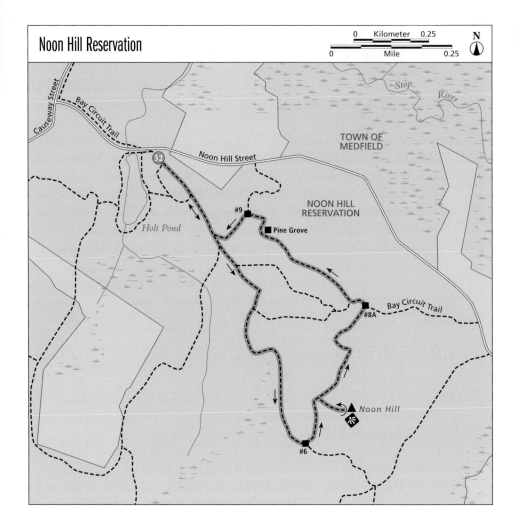

Noon Hill Reservation

0   Kilometer   0.25

0   Mile   0.25

N

Causeway Street

Bay Circuit Trail

32

Noon Hill Street

Holt Pond

#9

Pine Grove

TOWN OF
MEDFIELD

NOON HILL
RESERVATION

Stop River

#8A   Bay Circuit Trail

Noon Hill

#6

1.4   As soon as you see a #9 marker up ahead on a tree, the trail
opens up into a pine grove.

1.7   After dead-ending at a T intersection (the completioin of
the loop), turning right, and retracing your steps, you'll
return to the parking area.

Blue Hills Reservation: Great Blue Hill

This green-blazed loop encircles the Great Blue Hill section of Blue Hills Reservation lands. Often covering the lesser-traveled stretches, you'll also experience a spur along the Skyline Trail scrambling up steep rock leading to the shell of an old stone dwelling and tower high up on a ridge with horizon views. Terrain ranges from rock ridges and vernal pools to wide-open mature pine groves. Explanations for the name Blue Hills range from the type of granite that figures so prominently along the route to the bluish tint of the foliage when viewed from afar.

Start: Far corner of the Trailside Museum parking lot
Nearest town: Canton
Distance: 3.2-mile loop
Approximate hiking time: 2 hours
Difficulty: Moderate to difficult
Trail surface: Gravel access roads, packed earth, rock
Seasons: Year-round
Other trail users: Anglers, horseback riders, snowshoers, mountain bikers
Canine compatibility: Dogs on leash permitted

Land status: Department of Conservation and Recreation
Fees and permits: None
Schedule: Open dawn to dusk daily
Maps: On signboard and at www.mass.gov/dcr/parks/metroboston/blue%20hills%20brochure.pdf
Trail contacts: Department of Conservation and Recreation, 251 Causeway Street, Suite 600, Boston, MA 02114-2104; (617) 626-1250

Finding the trailhead: From I-93, take exit 2B onto Route 138 north. Travel approximately 1 mile until reaching the parking lot to your right that's just beyond the Trailside Museum entrance. GPS: N42 13.2184/W71 7.1102

Begin at the parking lot that's beyond the museum entrance, which doubles as the visitor center to your right. A stream parallels the front edge of this parking lot within the woods. Instead of embarking on the red trailhead with a map board that's readily apparent to your right at the edge of the parking lot, head to the far upper left-hand side of the parking lot as you're standing looking at the woods with your back to Route 138. Begin on a trap rock footpath with a small stream paralleling the trail to your right, which you'll eventually cross on a wooden footbridge. Shortly you'll curve up onto the paved Summit Road and walk up through a stand of pine, where you want to turn left off the pavement onto a level and wide dirt road passing through a sizable pine forest. Small plastic green circles nailed to the trees confirm that you're on the green trail loop.

Continuing over trap rock and larger stones on a flat grade, you'll see a field off to your left through a mix of pine, oak, and small beech. The trail bed is flat and wide until you turn left onto the Wolcott Path and walk down away from the established roadbed, passing through a wooded marsh with swamp maple and underbrush on either side. Even though the trail remains wide, the surface has transitioned from gravel to dirt. Soon you'll be fully removed from the marshy terrain, curving through stately pine, and able to see quite a way into the distance ahead.

Large trailside boulders

As you cross a dirt road, you'll see a signboard along with another small white sign with black lettering labeled 1114. Here you will continue south along Rotch Path toward Houghton's Pond through pine forest; you'll also witness that heavily trafficked portions of the trail intersect more remote stretches like the one you're now on quite abruptly, making for an interesting juxtaposition.

The terrain becomes more rugged as you begin climbing the gravel access road that now curves and cuts up into the hillside. After gaining some elevation, the trail soon levels out, and you'll pass a few large boulders immediately to your right. Here you'll be up on a ridge within the forest and be able to see a bit of the horizon down through small to medium pine into the distance.

Turning left onto the Blue Trail spur, also a portion of the Skyline Trail, you will depart a relatively level ramble to decidedly more challenging terrain cutting up a steep hill via stone steps carved into the rock ledge. As you look up vertically, it at first appears that these stones are in a haphazard jumble, but if you look down toward your feet as you're climbing, there is clearly a method to their arrangement into remarkably well-formed steps. After departing the rock stairs, you'll be walking on a ledge along with tumbled stone that hasn't been strategically altered.

You'll begin to get your first real views to your left through scrub pine up on a ridge. As you continue climbing, the blue markings continue on the rock surface at different intervals as well as on the trees. Soon you'll reach the top of Great Blue Hill, elevation 635 feet. Here you can explore Eliot Tower and Memorial Bridge, which are solidly constructed with stone. Although it appears that the two structures are one and the same, the bridge was actually built first in 1904 in memory of Charles Eliot, landscape architect for the Metropolitan Park Commission. A stone dwelling containing picnic tables as well as the attached 35-foot tower were built in 1933 by the Civilian Conservation Corps.

After exploring this work of craftsmanship and enjoying some skyline views, retrace your steps back down the hill continuing on the Green Trail.

Soon, you'll head over a pass with steep rock on either side, passing a small kettle pond to your right before turning left at a three-way intersection and continuing on a rugged wood road, completing the loop. Return to the trailhead the way you came.

> **☙ Green Tip:**
> *Go out of your way to avoid birds and animals*
> *that are mating or taking care of their young.*

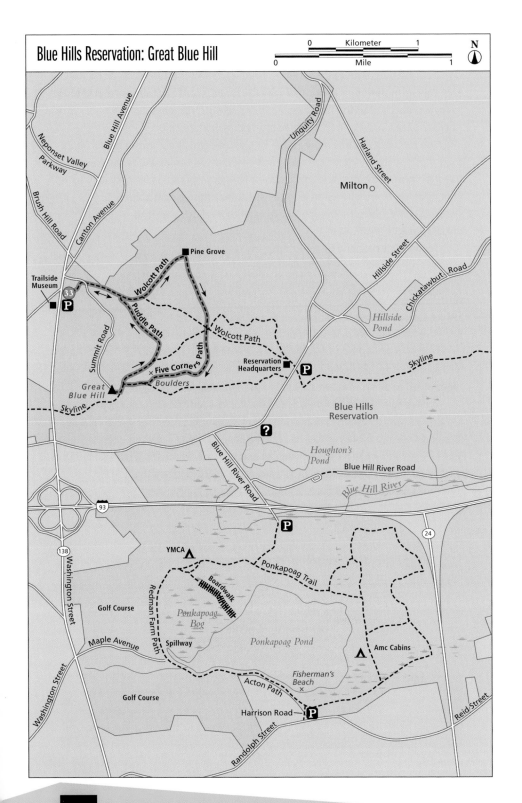

0   Kilometer   1

0   Mile   1

N

Neponset Valley Parkway

Blue Hill Avenue

Brush Hill Road

Canton Avenue

Unquity Road

Milton

Harland Street

Hillside Street

Chickatawbut Road

Trailside Museum

33

P

Pine Grove

Wolcott Path

Puddle Path

Summit Road

Wolcott Path

Hillside Pond

Five Corners Path

Reservation Headquarters

P

Skyline

Boulders

Great Blue Hill

Skyline

Blue Hills Reservation

?

Houghton's Pond

Blue Hill River Road

Blue Hill River Road

Blue Hill River

93

138

Washington Street

YMCA

Redman Farm Path

Golf Course

Maple Avenue

Ponkapoag Bog

Boardwalk

Spillway

Ponkapoag Trail

Ponkapoag Pond

24

Amc Cabins

Fisherman's Beach

Acton Path

P

Golf Course

Harrison Road

Randolph Street

Reid Street

0.0   Head to the far upper left-hand side of the parking lot as you're standing looking at the woods with your back to Route 138.

0.1   Turn left off the paved Summit Road onto a level and wide dirt road, passing through a sizable pine forest.

0.4   Continue straight through a trail intersection on the Green Trail.

0.5   Turn left onto the Wolcott Path.

0.7   Turn left at another trail intersection, continuing to follow green markings just after crossing a brook.

0.9   Turn right, curving through stately pine now fully away from marshy terrain.

1.0   Continue straight through a four-way intersection on the more established access road.

1.3   Cross a dirt road at an intersection with a signboard.

1.6   Turn right at a four-way intersection, continuing to follow the green blazes.

1.7   Pass a few large boulders immediately to your right where the trail levels out up on a ridge.

1.8   Fork to the right at an intersection, continuing to follow the green-blazed access road.

1.9   Turn left onto the blue trail, which is a portion of the Skyline Trail, cutting up a steep hill via stone steps carved into the rocky terrain.

2.0   Begin experiencing your first views to your left through scrub pine up on a ridge.

2.1   Reach the top of Great Blue Hill, where you'll be able to explore what used to be a stone house.

2.4   Turn left at a three-way intersection, continuing on the green-blazed access road.

3.2   After retracing your steps, return back to the parking lot.

Blue Hills Reservation: Ponkapoag Pond

Another hike within the vast Blue Hills Reservation land, this is a route of interesting extremes. On one end of Ponkapoag Pond is an Appalachian Mountain Club (AMC) encampment, while on the opposite end, the trail passes through a verdant golf course. Within minutes you can be deep in the pine forest losing your thoughts in nature, or just as quickly be skirting patches of heavy residential presence through the trees.

Start: Parking area off Randolph Street

Nearest town: Canton

Distance: 4.4-mile loop

Approximate hiking time: 2 hours

Difficulty: Easy

Trail surface: Packed earth with some gravel

Seasons: Year-round

Other trail users: Anglers, snowshoers, horseback riders, mountain bikers, paddle boaters

Canine compatibility: Dogs allowed on leash

Land status: Massachusetts Department of Conservation and Recreation

Fees and permits: None

Schedule: Dawn to dusk daily

Maps: Available at trailhead and online at www.mass.info/state .ma/recreation.htm

Trail contacts: Department of Conservation and Recreation, 251 Causeway Street, Suite 600, Boston, MA 02114-2104; (617) 626-1250

Finding the trailhead: From I-93/Route 128, take exit 2 onto Washington Street/Route 138 and continue south about 2 miles to Randolph Street, which is the next intersection after passing the golf course to your left. Turn left onto Randolph Street; the parking area is to your left just under a mile up a steep hill in the woods. GPS: N42 11.2091/W71 5.5814

THE HIKE

Begin from the parking area off Randolph Street, which is really a series of alcoves on a potholed gravel access road surrounded by wooden guardrails. Walk eastward down a hill on this road, and you'll begin to catch glimpses of the pond through the trees. Once on the Ponkapoag Trail, you'll pass through low-lying swampy woods on either side. Even though you're on a well-graded sand and gravel access road, the surface can get muddy during spring or after significant precipitation.

Some large elms surround the trail along with swampy underbrush continuing to your left before this access road opens up into a meadow with houses to your right visible through the woods line. Head down through this meadow, and just before turning back into the cover of forest, you'll see a marshy area straight ahead marked with a gas pipeline sign.

Continuing on this wooded access road, you'll pass through swamp maple and wooded marsh on either side before climbing a bit higher on this elevated roadbed away from wetland into pines and passing some brown Appalachian Mountain Club camp cabins to your left. After forking down away from the AMC camp on what is now a green-blazed access road, you'll pass a pump house to your right. Down to your left is swamp bordering the pond shore where you'll get

Ponkapoag Pond

seasonal water views through the trees. Even though you're now on a footpath traversing a ridge through oak and pine, it's well established and looks as if it may have been a wood road at one time.

Once you return to a graded gravel access road open to traffic, be vigilant for vehicles coming from behind. Head down on a slight but steady grade and then level out with wooded marsh on either side before heading into a thick pine forest, where you'll see a sign for the Ponkapoag YMCA Outdoor Center driveway to your right. To your left under a map board, a sign points to where you want to turn left on a trail spur leading to the quaking bog boardwalk. Pass straight though a clearing amidst towering pine and then onto a short footpath, where you'll quickly reach the boardwalk entrance to your left down a short steep hill marked with a stone monument commemorating those who aided in its maintenance over the years. Logs split lengthwise serve as planks carrying you right to water level for close-up exploration of this unique ecosystem.

Once you retrace your steps back to the main access road and continue proceeding through pine forest, you'll emerge into a golf course on a stone dust golf cart road and join caddies and duffers on their way to the back nine. This road skirts the back edge of the greens with the woods line directly to your left. Continue straight, cutting back under the cover of thick evergreens and paralleling the golf course to your right through a band of trees and underbrush with marsh views to your left.

As you move away from the golf course over a trap rock–surfaced dam similar to a breakwater constructed with large stones, the pond shore will be increasingly closer to your left. You'll cross over a spillway with the pond shore directly to your left until continuing straight off the trap rock surface onto a dirt road surrounded by pine forest. You'll also be headed away from being directly on the pond shore, but you'll continue on a level grade close to the pond with views through the trees to your left. Soon, you'll see houses close by to your right and then return to the signboard you first encountered on the route, completing the loop.

MILES AND DIRECTIONS

0.0 Begin from the parking lot down a gravel access road lined with wooden guardrails.

0.1 Pass through a metal gate down to a four-way trail intersection with a signboard straight ahead. Start by hiking in an easterly direction to walk the loop counterclockwise.

0.2 Turn left onto a more established dirt road graded well enough for automobile traffic.

0.4 Emerge into a meadow with residential presence up to your right.

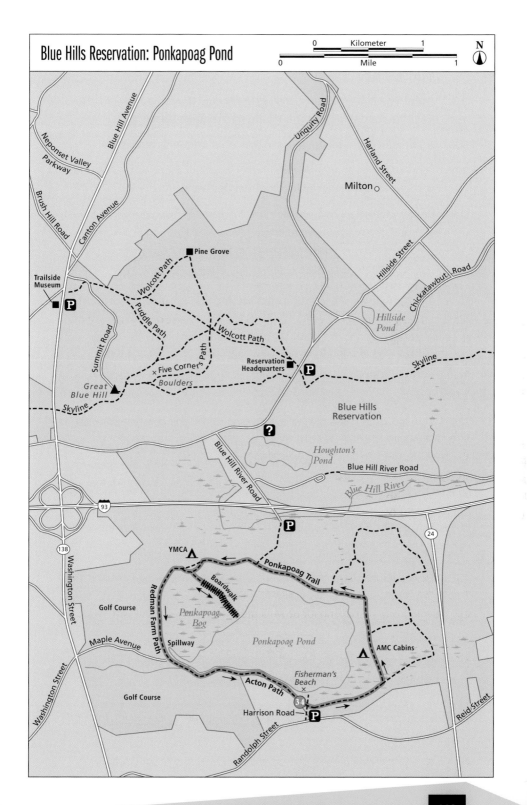

Blue Hills Reservation: Ponkapoag Pond

0.6 Climb a bit higher on this elevated roadbed away from the wooded marsh into pines.

0.7 Depart the AMC camp area, forking to the right down the access road away from the pond shore and continuing on the green-blazed trail.

0.8 Go straight past a pump house to your right through a pine grove.

0.9 Turn left (west) at another fork in the trail off an access road onto a foot-path surface covered with leaves rather than sand and gravel.

1.0 Cross a railroad tie bridge over a small stream tumbling through a marshy area and into a pond to your left.

1.5 Pass an unpainted metal gate to your left, reaching an intersection, where you'll want to turn left onto a well-graded gravel access road

1.9 Reach a four-way intersection after passing through a thick pine forest.

2.0 Begin on a boardwalk through the quaking bog.

2.4 Turn around at pond to rewalk boardwalk back to dirt access road.

2.8 Pass around a metal gate within the pine forest. Turn left to return to main trail.

2.9 Turn left (south) sharply upon emerging into a golf course, and continue along a stone dust golf cart road.

3.1 Continue straight, cutting back under the cover of thick evergreen trees and paralleling the golf course to your right through a band of trees and underbrush.

3.4 Pass a map board to your left as the trail bed continues to be level.

3.6 Cross over a spillway with the pond shore directly to your left.

3.7 Head straight off the trap rock surface and curve to the southeast back into the woods, surrounded by pine on a dirt road.

3.9 Pass houses close by to your right along with the pond shore visible to your left.

4.3 Return to the four-way intersection with signboard to your left and turn right, retracing your steps.

4.4 Arrive back at the parking area.

The Quaking Bog

Resting on a glacial kettle hole, a depression made when a huge block of ice buried in the ground eventually melted 12,000 to 14,000 years ago, a bog was formed. As plants decay and settle to the bottom, they decay extremely slowly, forming thick organic peat. Also contributing to peat accumulation is sphagnum moss, which rings the bog and eventually decays. This moss, very spongy and absorbent, was first used by natives to line their babies' diapers and later used as dressing for wounds.

Some interesting plants call this bog home, including the sundew and pitcher plants, which prey on insects in a way similar to a Venus flytrap. The pitcher plant attracts insects with fluids that collect in its hollow leaves. Tiny hairs on these leaves block the insect's escape, and enzymes help digest them. Pitcher plants have a red flower hanging from the center of green or purplish pitcher-shaped leaves and can reach 24 inches tall. Closer to the ground, the sundew has round leaves with white or pink flowers. Sticky fluid traps insects, and the plants leaves close around them, acquiring nutrients like nitrogen, which are scarce in the bog.

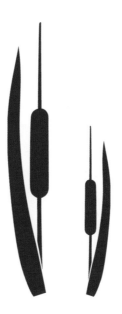

Borderland State Park

This route encompasses a diverse mix of recreational uses. You can whiz along this route on a bike, play a competitive game of disc golf in a tournament, head down one of the many side trails in wooded tranquility, or do all of the above within a single afternoon. All this plus two lovely ponds that offer boating, fishing, and swimming add up to plenty of opportunities for passive escape and more formalized recreation.

Start: Borderland State Park Visitors Center to the right of map signboard
Nearest town: North Easton
Distance: 3.1-mile loop
Approximate hiking time: 1.5 hours
Difficulty: Easy
Trail surface: Sand, gravel access roads, and grass
Seasons: Year-round
Other trail users: Birders, anglers, snowshoers, mountain bikers, paddle boaters, disc golfers
Canine compatibility: Dogs must be leashed

Land status: Department of Conservation and Recreation
Fees and permits: Entrance fee at parking lot kiosk
Schedule: 8:00 a.m. to sunset daily
Maps: On signboard at trailhead and at www.mass.gov/dcr/parks /borderland/downloads/Border lndTrailMap.pdf
Trail contacts: Visitors Center, 259 Massapoag Avenue, North Easton, MA 02356; (508) 238-6566

Finding the trailhead: From I-95 take exit 10, Norwood Street (Route 27). Turn left, driving through the traffic lights in Sharon Center. Go straight through this intersection and immediately bear right onto Pond Street. Follow Pond Street for 1.5 miles until you come to a traffic rotary. Go halfway around the rotary, continuing onto Massapoag Avenue for 3 miles to the park entrance on your left. As soon as you drive into the main entrance, continue past your first parking lot straight ahead overlooking the meadow and continue down the driveway toward the second and larger parking lot fronting the visitor center. GPS: N42 3.7847 / W71 9.7400

THE HIKE

This is a true multiuse trail that accommodates jogging, horseback riding, and trail bike riding along miles of level terrain. Take the Leach Pond Trail to the right of the visitor center on a level stone dust access road surrounded by mostly oak and pine. Walk eastward to hike the loop clockwise. You'll soon realize that disc golf is popular along this route because there are stations off in the woods at different intervals. You'll pass an access road to your right, which leads down to the pond shore, and a little past this point you'll see a stone lodge to your right overlooking Leach Pond. From here the trail bed curves close up along the pond shore with only a narrow band of underbrush separating you from the water's edge. Wooded marsh will now be to your left, populated with mostly oak.

You'll periodically pass trail signs to your left pointing to side trails, but continue straight on the main trail as it parallels the pond shore. You'll see a spillway to your right where a wooden bridge crosses below it, separating Upper Leach Pond from Lower Leach Pond. There is also a bench overlooking the waterfront at this intersection. Continue straight, and here the trail bed climbs up a steady grade onto a knoll further removed above the pond shore and overlooking Upper Leach Pond, which is ringed by marshland. The trail continues gaining and receding on subsequent knolls. Cross a brook that empties into the pond to your right. After

Lower Leach Pond views

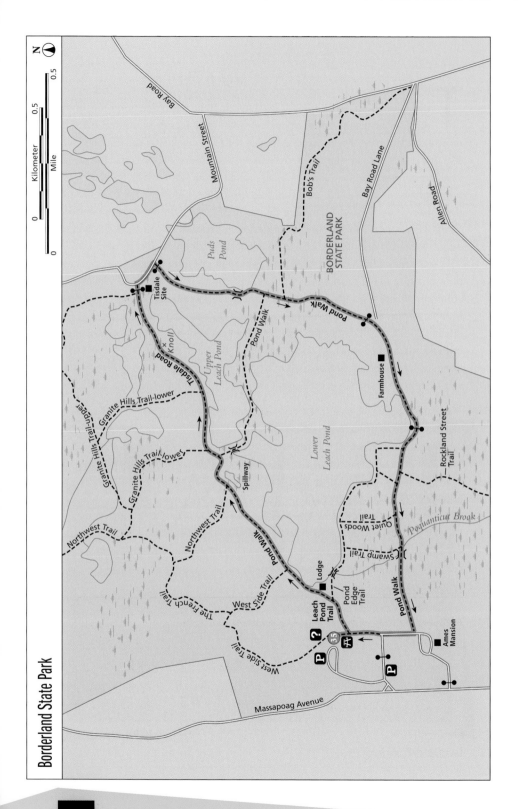

passing beneath some cedars arching over the trail, you'll arrive at a signboard titled CHANGING LANDSCAPES, CHANGING FAMILIES, which examines the different families that occupied what was once an estate over the years. You'll pass a stone bench to your right overlooking Upper Leach Pond before the trail intersects paved Mountain Street. After following this road for a bit, you'll be paralleling the pond once again, but this time to your right through the trees.

Soon you will see Puds Pond to your left through the trees as well. Follow the two wheel tracks after emerging into a long open meadow marking the trail bed across the grass. Cedar and pine along with other deciduous growth in the mixed border each side of the field in the distance. Soon you'll pass over a spillway and small dam separating Puds Pond to your immediate left with Upper Leach Pond to your right. This is a scenic spot for water views. After crossing, you'll continue into another meadow, this one more expansive and much more wide open than the last, on an almost perfectly level walking surface.

Meadow walking continues to follow the wheel tracks, and the field eventually curves to the right. In the distance a band of trees separates this expanse of grass from what is now Lower Leach Pond. As soon as the trail bed transitions back to an access road with a signboard and white farmhouse to your right, turn right back onto a level dirt access road bordered by a split rail fence on either side. To your right the meadow continues with the pond farther off in the distance. Pass through a brown metal gate; here the split rails end and the pond shore now meets the trail bed immediately to your right. The next major transition point is where you'll depart the water's edge to your right, heading into dense pine forest for a long stretch straight ahead on this flat access road. The pine forest gets deeper as you progress with many of the trees noticeably larger than elsewhere on the route. You'll quickly cross a concrete bridge over a brook and emerge into a meadow once again, this time containing a stone mansion to your left. Turn right here, continuing to follow the access road underneath some large oaks, until you complete the loop back at the visitor center.

MILES AND DIRECTIONS

0.0 Start on the Leach Pond Trail beginning to the right of the visitor center at the head of the large paved parking lot.

0.2 Continue past an access road leading down to Leach Pond to your right.

0.7 Pass a spillway spanned by a wooden bridge to your right, which separates Upper Leach Pond from Lower Leach Pond.

0.8 Continue straight onto Tisdale Road, as Pond Walk turns to the right to pass between the upper and lower ponds.

1.1 Traverse a knoll surrounded by pine and large oak. Turn right onto Mountain Street.

1.3 Cross a brook emptying into Upper Leach Pond to your right.

1.4 Turn right off Mountain Street behind a brown metal gate onto a wooded access road.

1.5 Emerge into a meadow, following two wheel tracks marking the trail bed across the grass.

1.6 Cross over a spillway and small dam separating Puds Pond to your immediate left with Upper Leach Pond to your right.

2.0 Turn right onto an access road with a signboard and white farmhouse to your right.

2.3 Pass through a brown metal gate. Here the split rails end, and the pond shore now meets the trail bed immediately to your right.

2.4 Depart the water's edge to your right, heading into dense pine.

2.8 Cross a concrete bridge over a brook, continuing under the cover of pine.

3.0 Turn right with a stone mansion to your left surrounded by meadow.

3.1 Complete the loop by continuing northward along an access road surrounded by large oak and return to the visitor center.

> **🌰 Green Tip:**
> *Minimize the use and impact of fires.*
> *Use designated fire spots or existing fire rings (if permitted).*
> *When building fires, use small sticks (less than 1 ½ inches in diameter) that you find on the ground. Keep your fire small, burn it to ash, put it out completely, and scatter the cool ashes. If you can, it's best to avoid making a fire at all.*

Wheaton Farm Conservation Area

In addition to some good birding opportunities along the wooded edges of a large meadow and some good portions of the trail bed generously carpeted in pine needles, the two ponds on either side of the beginning of this route are well known by local anglers for their bountiful bass. So bring your binoculars and fishing pole to this lesser-known wildlife preserve.

Start: Behind the telephone pole railing at head of the parking lot
Nearest town: Easton
Distance: 1.5-mile loop
Approximate hiking time: 1 hour
Difficulty: Easy
Trail surface: Packed earth, gravel access road
Seasons: Year-round
Other trail users: Birders, anglers, snowshoers, cross-country skiers

Canine compatibility: Dogs allowed
Land status: Town of Easton Conservation Land
Fees and permits: None
Schedule: Dawn to dusk daily
Maps: New England Topo quad
Trail contacts: Easton Conservation Commission; 136 Elm Street, North Easton, MA 02356; (508) 230-0530

Finding the trailhead: From I-495, take exit 9 and follow Bay Street north toward Easton for 3.2 miles. The parking lot entrance is extremely easy to miss, but the key landmark to look for is a Federalist-style barn to your right. In front of this barn will be a brown sign with white lettering indicating the historical background of the structure. Directly across the street is where you want to turn left, pass through a brown metal gate, and head down a dirt driveway. The dirt driveway curves down into a parking area fronted by a telephone pole railing. GPS: N42 0.3148/W71 7.3553

After passing what appears to be a pump house up to your left, you'll first pass a marshy pond directly to your right through the trees. Once you cross a short concrete bridge spanning the marshy pond to your right and a longer and larger pond to your left, you'll get a good perspective as to why this area is so good for birding. Plenty of marsh grass and cattails fringe the shore, providing nesting and protective covering. This combined with ample shallows provide excellent feeding grounds for blue herons. They snap up frogs and minnows with their long bills, tip back their heads, and swallow them whole.

Continue on this level, gravelly access road that forms a dike between the two ponds surrounded by a band of underbrush on either side until turning left onto a wood road, which immediately passes into a stately pine forest. The trail is completely level, straight, surrounded by walls of thick pine, and carpeted with a lush layer of needles. As you progress, you'll catch glimpses of the pond through the trees to your left.

Trail bed view

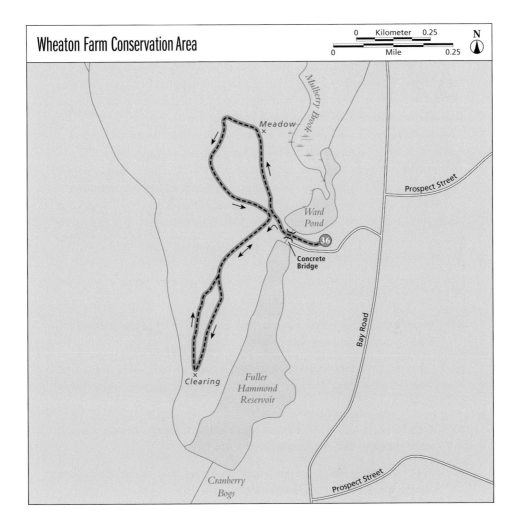

0   Kilometer   0.25

0   Mile   0.25

N

Mulberry Brook

Meadow ×

Prospect Street

Ward Pond

36

Concrete Bridge

Bay Road

× Clearing

Fuller Hammond Reservoir

Cranberry Bogs

Prospect Street

You'll soon pass a metal shed to your left and notice that you're headed in the direction of the pond shore visible straight ahead through the trees. You'll also see covered concrete shafts sticking out of the ground sporadically on either side of the trail. Now you are getting clearer pond views to the left through the trees with the forest increasingly opening up until you reach a clearing where you are now on a point in the woods extending into the pond. This spot makes for more excellent birding since this area is secluded and you have broad water views. Chances are good that you'll see mute swans in addition to other waterfowl. Despite their graceful and majestic appearance, these birds are an invasive species from Europe. They are extremely aggressive and territorial, driving away natives like the wood duck from their preferred nesting areas.

As soon as you depart this point, you'll be cutting back into deep pine on a narrower footpath surrounded by many small pine saplings crowding each side of the trail bed. After passing straight through two intersections that you previously crossed through, you'll notice the marshier pond you passed at the beginning of your hike now through the trees to your right, but you'll quickly curve to the left away from any water views into the wooded interior. You'll encounter your next nature-viewing opportunity when you reach the edge of a meadow. As you're paralleling it to your right alongside a stone wall and a band of trees, keep your eye out for deer and bluebirds, which love to nest at the edge of wooded meadows.

After turning left onto a footpath at a four-way intersection, you'll be passing through pitch pine until you complete the loop back between the ponds to the parking area. Pitch pines are readily distinguished from red and white pine by their sturdier and sharper needles.

MILES AND DIRECTIONS

0.0 Begin behind the telephone pole railing at the head of the parking lot, leading down into a red pine grove.

0.1 Cross a short concrete bridge spanning a pond on either side of the trail. Turn left onto a wood road at the first intersection, passing into a stately pine forest.

0.3 Curve sharply to the left, continuing to follow the more heavily traveled stone dust trail bed carpeted with pine needles.

0.5 Reach a clearing within the pine forest on a point close to the pond shore. Turn to the north to complete the loop.

1.1 The trail surface changes to a footpath just before entering a meadow.

1.2 Turn left at the major intersection onto a footpath passing through pitch pine.

1.3 Turn left back onto an established wood road.

1.4 Fork to the left again, completing the loop back at the first major intersection you encountered on the route. Retrace your streps to the southeast.

1.5 Arrive back at the trailhead.

Whitney and Thayer Woods

This route passes through diverse terrain ranging from pine-studded highlands to a brookside ramble through an extensive rhododendron and flowering shrub grove. Connecting this varied terrain are remarkably level and well-maintained carriage roads throughout much of the route, making for interesting and pleasant strolling during any season.

Start: Crushed stone access road to your right at the head of the parking lot

Nearest town: Hingham

Distance: 3.2-mile loop

Approximate hiking time: 1.5 hours

Difficulty: Easy

Trail surface: Packed earth, mowed grassland, sand, and gravel

Seasons: Year-round

Other trail users: Birders, snow-shoers, bikers

Canine compatibility: Dogs on leash permitted

Land status: Trustees of Reservations property

Fees and permits: None

Schedule: 8:00 a.m. to 6:00 p.m. Tues–Sun

Maps: At the trailhead and online at www.thetrustees.org/assets /documents/places-to-visit/trail maps/Whitney-and-Thayer-Woods -Weir-River-Farm-Trail-Map.pdf

Trail contacts: Trustees of Reservations, (781) 784-0567; seregion@ttor.org; www.the trustees.org

Finding the trailhead: From Route 3, take exit 14 and follow Route 228 north for 6.5 miles. Turn right onto Route 3A South and follow for 2 miles to the parking area entrance on your right. GPS: N42 14.0473 / W70 49.4568

Begin down a slight grade under some tall pines. You'll notice a telephone wire that leads to a private residence located off this road. As you continue passing under large pines, you'll notice that the roadbed is elevated above wooded marsh to your right. You'll soon transition up onto a rougher, less-traveled wood road through a mix of pine along with some holly and underbrush fringing the trail. As you're climbing at a slight but steady incline, you will pass sporadic glacially deposited boulders to either side of the trail within the woods. An extreme example is Bigelow Boulder, the size of an upturned car, which you'll pass immediately to your right.

You are on Boulder Lane once the trail bed is elevated above wooded marsh to your left with pine trees down an embankment to your right. The trail bed soon passes over wooded marsh on either side before gaining in elevation at a gradual but steady pitch. Once on Ayers Lane, you'll continue flat but elevated above the surrounding forest floor putting you on a knoll at different points within this segment of the route. As with so many acres of New England forest, you'll see a good number of stone walls within the woods. It's not difficult to surmise that these monuments to hard labor weren't always shrouded in trees. Originally the walls separated Colonial-era pastures; later they bordered the Whitney-Thayer lands (see

Trailside wooden bench for contemplation

sidebar), which served as woodlots. Today, they remind us of nature's regenerative power even in the face of human manipulation.

The trail suddenly narrows to a footpath, once you turn left on Milliken Memorial Path, and majestic rhododendrons crowd either side. To your left you'll see a metal commemorative plaque affixed to a stone. Bordering Wompatuck State Park, this memorial path was also planted with azaleas and other blooming shrubs in the late 1920s and dedicated by prominent Cohasset resident Arthur Milliken in memory of his wife, Mabel Minott Milliken.

As the rhododendrons get thicker, you'll be paralleling and crossing Brass Kettle Brook. At one point, you'll cross this brook on a wooden footbridge completely surrounded by lush vegetation. Before crossing, look to your left and you'll see a wooden bench ensconced in the greenery overlooking this serene scene. If it's not occupied, grab it for a few Zen moments.

Once you're back onto a wider gravel access road, you'll curve down a hill and cross a stone bridge over Brass Kettle Brook, which is in this portion deep and swift moving yet narrow, and marked with a telephone pole with a solar panel on top. Looking down into the water, you'll notice that a device is connected to the telephone pole: a micro hydro turbine harnessing the stream's currents.

Proceeding onward, you'll pass Rooster Rock to your right in the woods: a natural sculpture consisting of a big boulder propped up by a smaller one. Since there's nothing like it nearby, it really stands out. From here you'll be headed downward within the forest, and once it levels off completely, you'll pass around a green metal gate. Soon you'll pass a private residence to your right, and you'll then be walking along the driveway's roadbed and completing the loop retracing your steps back up the hill to the parking area.

Who Were Whitney and Thayer?

As agriculture declined throughout the nineteenth century, large properties were increasingly used for recreation. In 1904 local riding enthusiast Henry Whitney began assembling parcels to comprise a private estate for equestrian activities. Bridle trails and carriage roads were built. A horseback riding group called the Whitney Woods Association acquired more than 600 acres from Whitney, later donating them to the Trustees of Reservations. In 1943 the Trustees added Thayer to the reservation's name in honor of the wife of a former dean of Harvard Law School, Mrs. Ezra Ripley Thayer, who donated land west of the original parcel.

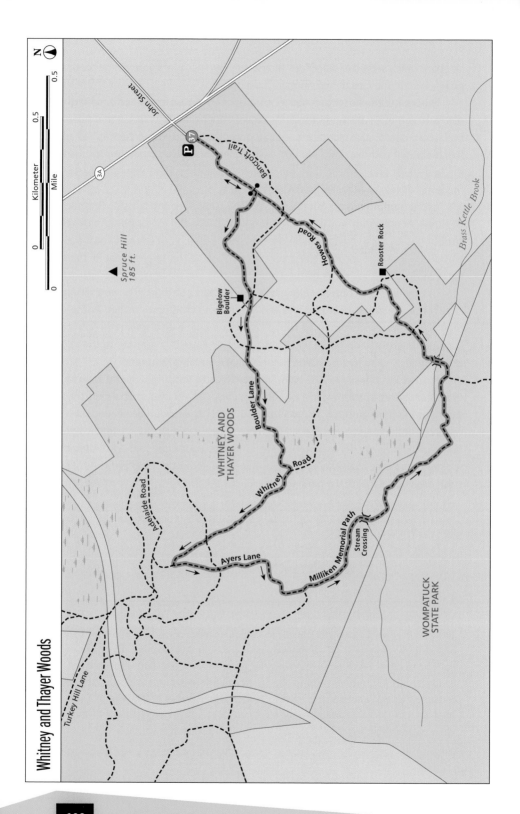

198 Inland Hikes

MILES AND DIRECTIONS

0.0 Begin at the head of the parking area with a map board containing give-away maps to your right.

0.3 Turn right past a green metal gate up onto a rougher, less traveled wood road.

0.5 Pass the Bigelow Boulder to your right, continuing straight past a trail intersecting to your left.

0.9 Curve to the right through this trail intersection onto Whitney Road, passing through notable pine stands.

1.3 Turn left onto Ayers Lane, continuing flat but elevated above the surrounding forest floor.

1.7 Stay left at a three-way intersection onto Milliken Memorial Path.

1.8 Pass over a stream coursing through small pipes underneath the trail.

2.0 Cross Brass Kettle Brook on a wooden foot-bridge surrounded by thick rhododendron.

2.3 Pass over a stream coursing through pipes underneath the trail.

2.4 Stay left at an intersection back onto a wider access road with a gravel surface.

2.6 Pass a big boulder propped up by a little boulder to your right in the woods.

2.7 Continue straight through a trail intersection where you'll now be completely level and pass through a green metal gate.

3.2 Return to the parking area after retracing your steps back up the sand and gravel access road.

While hiking this extensive loop on wooded access roads, you'll pass a large quarry with cliff views from atop. The route crosses Rattlesnake Brook, part of the Taunton watershed, twice along this route, providing some good seasonal trout-fishing opportunities. Be aware that you may be sharing the trail with motocross bikes as they are allowed on certain portions of this route.

Start: Rattlesnake Brook parking area at Freetown—Fall River State Forest

Nearest town: Assonet

Distance: 3-mile loop

Approximate hiking time: 2 hours

Difficulty: Moderate

Trail surface: Gravel access roads and some packed earth

Seasons: Year-round

Other trail users: Birders, anglers, snowshoers, mountain bikers, ATV users

Canine compatibility: Dogs allowed

Land status: Department of Conservation and Recreation

Fees and permits: None

Schedule: Dawn to dusk daily

Maps: Available at www.mass .gov/dcr/parks/trails/print/Free twnFallR.pdf

Trail contacts: Department of Conservation and Recreation, 251 Causeway Street, Suite 600, Boston, MA 02114-2104; (617) 626-1250

Finding the trailhead: Take exit 9 from Route 24, traveling south on South Main Street. Follow South Main Street for approximately 0.5 mile and turn left onto Copicut Road. Follow until it ends at a T intersection with Bell Rock Road. Turn right onto Bell Rock Road and follow it a little over 0.5 mile, where you'll see a dirt parking lot to your right surrounded by metal guardrails. GPS: N41 45.5371 / W71 4.3066

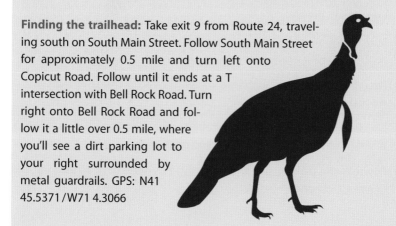

THE HIKE

Begin at the trailhead, passing through an opening in tire-wrapped metal guardrails that border the parking lot. You'll be on a sandy footpath well worn by ATV traffic and surrounded by small pitch pines. As soon as you pass a rusted gate mostly hidden by trees to your left, turn left across from Ledge Road. The trail bed continues onto a wider sandy access road through many pine saplings as well as medium dead oak. Soon the access road widens, appearing to have once accommodated larger vehicles. The trail bed cuts deeply into the forest floor as you progress downward on a slight but steady pitch.

Depending on the season and rainfall, a brook crosses the trail without the benefit of a drainage pipe or bridge to help you traverse it. Be prepared to step over stones on this lower-lying portion. You'll notice ATV symbols on the trees, giving you an official reminder that this type of trail user may be joining you. Continue on the sand and gravel access road now surrounded by a mix of different size pitch pine. Some trees are larger yet in the distance and not looming over the trail, making it wide open and bright.

After passing around a brown metal gate and turning left at a wide four-way intersection, you'll be on a well-graded sand and gravel access road that any vehicle, including a car, would be able to traverse. Steadily descending and then leveling off, you'll cross Rattlesnake Brook over a substantial stone bridge that appears to

View of Granite Quarry below

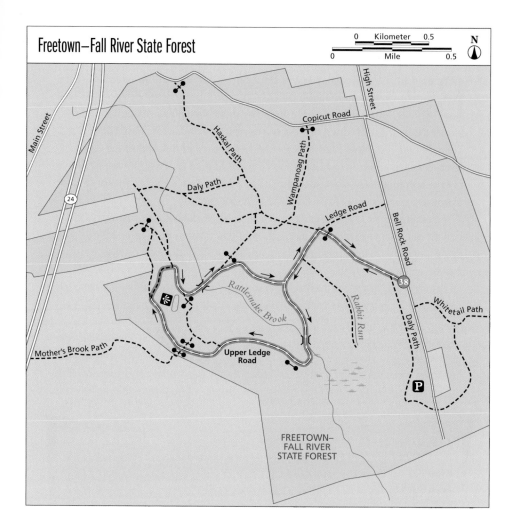

be built from choice stone extracted from a quarry (which you'll soon pass) when it was in operation during the early twentieth century. Nearby Fall River was famous for its solid architecture built from local granite quarries during this time period.

After you round a corner and pass a brown metal gate with red markings that fronts a footpath to your left, you'll cross a small brook running underneath the roadbed through a culvert. Here you'll begin a long, steady climb over a noticeably more gravelly and stony trail surface. Only when you see a rock outcropping rising up from the forest floor through the woods leading to a ridge to your left will you level off, surrounded by mostly scrub oak. After climbing a slight but prolonged and steady grade, you'll be high up above an abandoned quarry filled with water far below on a large rock cliff, which is accessible to your right. This area would be perfect for lingering and enjoying the views, but trash and graffiti left over from less considerate trail users mar the scenery. Here you need to carefully look for a footpath to your left as you stand facing the quarry down below in order to continue the route.

Once on this path, you'll pass through underbrush with ledge-bordering steep cliffs directly to your right. Follow the path steeply downward. While erosion bars are built into the hillside, they're not particularly successful at preventing erosion. You'll quickly intersect a gravel access road once again at the bottom of the quarry, where you'll see a brown metal gate to your right. Cross Rattlesnake Brook over a small bridge farther down, and continue on the more established access road through a mix of small and large pine. Soon after passing a sandpit to your left through the trees, you'll complete the loop back at the T intersection you encountered earlier marked with the brown signs. This time you are coming from Ledge Road. From here, turn left, retracing your steps back to the parking area.

MILES AND DIRECTIONS

0.0 Trailhead begins to the left of a signboard at the far corner of the parking lot surrounded by metal guardrails.

0.2 Cross a brook.

0.4 Turn left at a large four-way intersection onto a wide sand and gravel access road (Ledge Road).

0.6 Bear left at a T intersection onto the Upper Ledge Trail.

0.9 Cross Rattlesnake Brook over a substantial stone bridge.

1.1 Continue past a brown metal gate with red markings fronting a footpath to your left.

1.3 Pass over a small brook running underneath the roadbed through a culvert.

1.5 Pass a rock outcropping rising up from the forest floor up on a ridge to your left.

1.8 Reach an overlook high on a rock cliff above an abandoned quarry filled with water.

2.0 Cross Rattlesnake Brook over a small bridge.

2.1 Fork to the right, continuing on a more established access road.

2.3 Pass a sandpit to your left.

3.0 After retracing your steps, return back to the parking area.

Destruction Brook Woods Preserve

Located near historic Russell Mills in Dartmouth, this preserve once contained an active farmstead and millworks. Although enveloped in the deep woods, remnants of long-ago human habitation are clearly evident along this route preserved much like it was in the 1600s when the area was first settled.

Start: From the small dirt turnoff, head straight down a well-worn footpath toward a map board to your left in the woods

Nearest town: Dartmouth

Distance: 3.7-mile double loop

Approximate hiking time: 2.5 hours

Difficulty: Moderate

Trail surface: Packed earth

Seasons: Year-round

Other trail users: Birders, snowshoers, horseback riders

Canine compatibility: Dogs permitted

Land status: Dartmouth Natural Resources Trust

Fees and permits: None

Schedule: Sunrise to sunset daily

Maps: Available at www.dnrt.org /pdfs/dbwmapjan07.jpg

Trail contacts: Dartmouth Natural Resources Trust, P.O. Box P17, 404 Elm Street, Dartmouth, MA 02748; (508) 991-2289; info@dnrt.org

Finding the trailhead: From I-195, take exit 11 toward US 6/Dartmouth, merging onto Reed Road, and follow it approximately 2 miles. Turn right onto Beeden Road, continuing 0.7 mile, and then turn right onto Old County Road. Turn left onto Fisher Road. A white Dartmouth Natural Resources Trust sign with green lettering marks a small dirt turnoff to your right just before reaching the intersection of Fisher and Woodcock Roads. GPS: N41 34.7664/W71 0.9530

THE HIKE

After turning left at your first four-way intersection a short way in from Fisher Road, you'll be on a well-worn old carriage roadbed paralleling Fisher Road for a stretch, seeing the backs of houses through the trees to your left. As you curve to the left onto more of a footpath into larger pine and a wider open forest floor, you'll still see houses to the left through the trees.

You'll be climbing up a hill with some particularly large pine to your right. At the next T intersection with yellow markings that you'll reach after a quick climb through a pine grove, turn right, continuing your climb up on a ridge rising within the forest floor. As you continue following the yellow markings, you'll be on a level but somewhat wet trail bed surrounded by wooded marsh populated with swamp maple and some pine.

Soon you'll cross Destruction Brook, a small stream that passes underneath the trail through a pipe. It's hard to imagine that a gristmill was established in this vicinity around 1690 because now, depending on the season, water may not be flowing through at all. In the distance to your right through the trees, you'll see a small circular marsh surrounded by thicket. As you continue winding through smaller pines then progress into a larger, more established pine grove, you'll reach a higher elevation from the rest of the forest floor, making for more scenic views than before.

After passing a small dam to your right, cross a small concrete bridge, and then pass a wooden gate to your left at the head of a trail. After turning right at a

Destruction Brook trailhead

T intersection, you'll soon pass a large boulder with an old mill pond through the trees to your right. Here the trail bed is sandy and elevated above the rest of the forest floor with the small pond and eventually slow-moving Destruction Brook visible through the trees to your right.

Once you reach a T intersection with Ella's Bridge to your right over a small wooden bridge, turn left, continuing on a level, mostly gravel and sand surface heading away from the brook through deciduous growth. Remain alert for wood thrushes in this area. You'll now be passing through deeper forest, winding up on a slight grade curving up through mostly smaller oak and pine. Once you reach a pine ridge, you'll be traversing it within the forest for a good distance, experiencing broad views of the forest floor below.

Eventually heading down to your left off this pine ridge, you'll cross a two-planked footbridge over a small stream and reach the edge of a sandpit, making a sharp left away from a derelict car that has endured numerous bouts of unauthorized target practice over the years. Soon after making another sharp left, the trail bed opens up into meadow mostly to your right with a stone wall. A residence will be visible to your right, and you'll be able to see quite far into the distance straight ahead alongside this meadow on a grassy trail surface.

After abruptly transitioning into thick forest, crossing a stream, and passing through a wooded marsh, a stone wall will be on either side leading up to an old farmstead site from the 1700s marked with a stone foundation visible to your right up through an opening in the stone wall in a clearing. A few steps farther you'll see

Foundations from the P. Russell Homestead

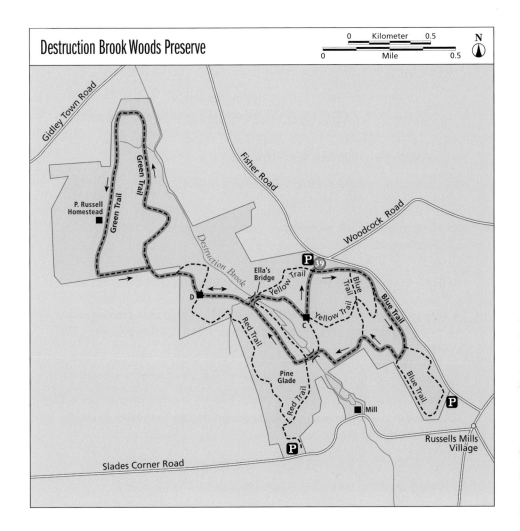

Destruction Brook Woods Preserve

on your left a stone barn foundation nicely intact and marked with two stone pillars.

You'll complete a loop within this route where you'll now be retracing your steps, continuing straight ahead until you turn left, crossing Ella's Bridge. Immediately fork to the right with the brook visible through underbrush to your right. Proceed through small and medium pine crowding the trail on either side, and soon you'll reconnect with the first four-way intersection you encountered on this route with Fisher Road and the parking turnoff now visible through the trees straight ahead.

MILES AND DIRECTIONS

0.0 Head straight down a well-worn footpath toward a map board to your left in the woods.

0.1   Turn left at a four-way intersection onto a well-worn carriage road paralleling Fisher Road through the trees to your left.

0.2   Curve slightly to the left and then proceed straight onto the Blue Trail, which is more of a footpath. You'll see a yellow and blue marking on a tree straight ahead.

0.4   Fork off to the right onto the Yellow Trail.

0.5   Turn to your left but not a sharp left at a three-way intersection, continuing to follow the yellow markings.

0.7   Continue to the left, following the yellow markings at a confusing four-way intersection.

0.9   Pass a large boulder and dammed-up portion of the brook through the trees to your right.

1.1   Turn left at a T intersection onto the Red Trail (the start of the second loop), continuing on a level sand and gravel wood road heading away from the brook.

1.3   Curve to the right down onto the Green Trail at a four-way intersection marked with a D on a stone in front of you.

1.4   Turn left at a T intersection, heading through thick pine and continuing to follow the green markings.

1.8   Pass through a stone wall up on a pine ridge within the forest.

2.0   Head down to your left off the pine ridge at a fork in the trail.

2.1   Turn left sharply away from a derelict junked car in a sandpit back into pine.

2.4   Cross a stream that passes underneath the trail through a stone sluice.

2.5   Pass an old farmstead site with the stone foundation from the P. Russell Homestead in a clearing to your right.

2.7   Turn left at a T intersection, continuing on the footpath with a residential presence through the trees to your right and a stone wall paralleling the trail to your left.

3.2   Turn left, cross Ella's Bridge, and then fork to the right away from the Yellow Trail alongside the brook visible through underbrush to your right.

3.45   Make a sharp left at intersection C with the Yellow Trail.

3.7   Return to the parking turnoff after passing the map board to your right.

Nasketucket Bay State Reservation

Once wide-open grazing land for sheep, the rolling meadowlands comprising this reservation provide bountiful natural habitat for wildflowers and migrating birds along Buzzards Bay. From nearby Fairhaven, Herman Melville embarked on the whaling expedition that would shape the classic Moby-Dick.

Start: From the head of the parking lot, pass through a stone wall and immediately turn right

Nearest town: Fairhaven

Distance: 1.8-mile double loop

Approximate hiking time: 1 hour

Difficulty: Easy

Trail surface: Sand, gravel, and packed earth

Seasons: Year-round

Other trail users: Birders, snowshoers

Canine compatibility: No dogs allowed

Land status: Massachusetts Department of Conservation and Recreation

Fees and permits: None

Schedule: Sunrise to sunset daily

Maps: Visit www.topo.com

Trail contacts: Department of Conservation and Recreation, 251 Causeway Street, Suite 600, Boston, MA 02114-2104; (617) 626-1250; mass.parks@state.ma.us

Finding the trailhead: From I-195 West, take the Fairhaven exit 18 onto Route 240 south for a short distance to traffic lights at Route 6. Turn left and travel east on Route 6 for five to ten minutes across the Fairhaven-Mattapoisett border. Turn right onto Brandt Island Road, bearing left at a fork and then curving right at a sign for Brandt Beach Road. Parking lot is to your right at the DEM sign.

From I-195 East, take the Mattapoisett exit 19, bearing right off the exit ramp onto North Street. Turn right at the first intersection with a traffic light onto Route 6 West, proceeding for several miles, crossing the Mattapoisett River Bridge and passing Mattapoisett Neck Road. Turn left onto Brandt Island Road. Follow Brandt Island Road, bearing left at a fork, curve right at sign for Brandt Beach Road, and park to the right at the DEM. GPS: N41 38.1365/W70 50.2204

After passing through the stone wall, you'll immediately turn right away from a trail map board to your left on a level stone dust trail surrounded by oak, swamp maple, tall grass, and small pine saplings on either side. Once a farm road, the trail bed is now bordered by a band of meadow on either side, which soon becomes wetter and more of a wooded marsh on either side within the trees. During spring, tall spikes of purple Veronica and, come July, bushes loaded with ripened blueberries populate and fringe the overgrown meadow grasses.

You'll soon reach an intersection marked with small brown signs with white lettering. Pointing to your right is the Meadow Trail, but you want to continue straight ahead on the Bridle Trail. Soon you'll round a corner as this access road opens up into a more wide-open meadow with small pine clustering on the left-hand side within the grass. Continue straight through another intersection, continuing on the Bridle Trail and passing by the Holly Trail to your left and a sign pointing to the Meadow Trail to your right, although there doesn't appear to be a footpath opening here.

Farther down the Bridle Trail, you'll pass the Salt Marsh Trail to your right, but continue ahead on the Bridle Trail with the small pine saplings and wide-open meadow grass continuing on either side. Turn left once you dead-end at a T intersection onto the Holly Trail, moving away from being surrounded by open

Looking past the trailhead

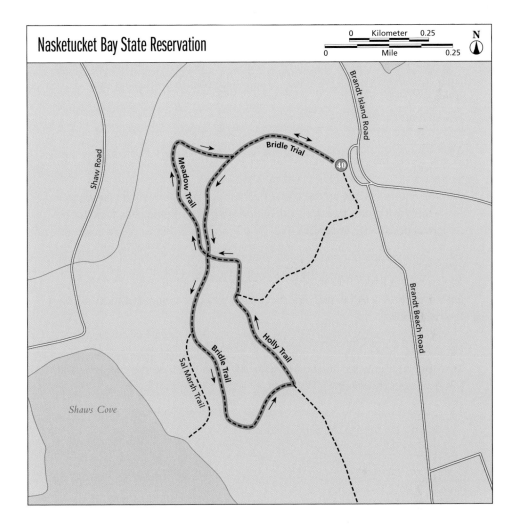

meadow into thick woods populated by mostly pine and holly. Some of these holly trees reach 20 feet in height and have 2-foot-wide trunks, testament to the fact that they have been thriving here for years. Portions of the trail bed can be wet in this spot depending on the season.

The trail bed continues flat and easygoing surrounded by wet, rugged terrain. Soon you'll intersect back with the Bridle Trail, where you want to continue straight and cross over onto the Meadow Trail. It's not readily apparent at first where the trail bed is but a little farther in you'll find it carving through the meadow with the woods line close up to your left and soon veer out into the open meadow to your right. You'll see a red barn off to your left on the horizon, giving a clear sign that there are still working farms in the vicinity. Stay alert for bluebirds and yellow warblers that thrive in this environment during spring nesting season. Once you reach the woods line, you'll depart the open meadow into marshy underbrush on a straight, flat, and grassy trail surface. Soon you'll reconnect with the Bridal Trail where you want to turn left and retrace your steps back to the parking area.

MILES AND DIRECTIONS

0.0 Pass through the stone wall at the head of the parking lot onto a stone dust trail.

0.2 Continue straight on the Bridle Trail through an intersection where you'll see small brown trail signs with white lettering pointing ahead and to the Meadow Trail to your right.

0.4 Continue straight on the Bridle Trail, passing by the Holly Trail to your left and a sign pointing to the Meadow Trail to your right.

0.6 Pass the Salt Marsh Trail intersection to your right, continuing ahead on the Bridle Trail.

0.9 Turn left at a T intersection onto the Holly Trail.

1.5 Depart from open meadow into marshy underbrush on a straight, flat, and grassy trail surface.

1.8 After turning left back onto the Bridle Trail, retrace your steps on the stone dust path back to the parking area.

> 🌱 **Green Tip:**
> *Cotton clothing has a smaller carbon footprint*
> *(when washed in cold water) than either polyester or wool.*

Appendix A: Land Use Management and Conservation Organizations

Massachusetts Audubon Society
208 South Great Road
Lincoln, MA 01773
(781) 259-9500
(800) AUDUBON
www.massaudubon.org

Essex County Greenbelt Association
82 Eastern Avenue
Essex, MA 01929
(978) 768-7241
ecga@ecga.org
www.ecga.org

Andover Village Improvement Society
P.O. Box 5097
Andover, MA 01810
info@avisandover.org
www.avisandover.org

Bay Circuit Alliance
3 Railroad Street
Andover, MA 01810
(978) 470-1982
baycircuit@juno.com
www.baycircuit.org

Charles River Conservancy
4 Brattle Street
Cambridge, MA 02138
(617) 608-1410
crc@thecharles.org
www.thecharles.org

Dartmouth Natural Resources Trust
PO Box P-17
Dartmouth, MA 02748
(508) 991-2289
info@dnrt.org
www.dnrt.org

Friends of Lynn Woods
P.O. Box 8216
Lynn, MA 01904
(781) 593-7773
www.flw.org

Manchester-Essex Conservation Trust
P.O. Box 1486
Manchester, MA 01944
conserve@mect.org
www.mect.org

Friends of the Middlesex Fells Reservation
78 Stone Place
Melrose, MA 02176
(781) 662-2340
friends@fells.org
www.fells.org

Trustees of Reservations
572 Essex Street
Beverly, MA 01915-1530
(978) 921-1944
information@ttor.org
www.thetrustees.org

Trust for Public Land
33 Union Street, Fourth Floor
Boston, MA 02108
(617) 367-6200
www.tpl.org

**Massachusetts Department of
Conservation and Recreation**
251 Causeway Street, Suite 600
Boston, MA 02114-2104
(617) 626-1250
mass.parks@state.ma.us
www.mass.gov/dcr

Appendix B: Hiking Clubs

Appalachian Mountain Club
Boston Chapter
5 Joy Street
Boston, MA 02108
(617) 523-0636
www.amcboston.org

Blue Hills Adult Walking Club
Department of Conservation and Recreation
Blue Hills Reservation
695 Hillside Street
Milton, MA 02186
(617) 698-1802, extension 3
www.mass.gov/dcr/events/blue hills walking club.pdf

Massachusetts Sierra Club
100 Boylston Street
Boston, MA 02116
(617) 423-5775
www.sierraclubmass.org

Breakheart-Fells Hiking Club
Download information at:
www.mass.gov/dcr/events/breakhwalks.pdf

Appendix C: Outdoor Outfitters

REI Boston
401 Park Drive
Boston, MA 02215
(617) 236-0746
Store hours: 10:00 a.m.–9:00 p.m.
Mon–Fri; 10:00 a.m.–9:00 p.m. Sat;
11:00 a.m.–6:00 p.m. Sun
www.rei.com

Hilton's Tent City
272 Friend Street
Boston, MA 02114
(617) 227-9242
Store hours: 9:00 a.m.–9:00 p.m. Mon–
Fri; 9:00 a.m.–6:00 p.m. Sat; noon–6:00
p.m. Sun
htc@hiltonstentcity.com
www.hiltonstentcity.com

Moor and Mountain
3 Railroad Street
Andover, MA 01810
(978) 475-3665
Store hours: 9:00 a.m.–5:00 p.m. Mon–
Wed and Sat; 9:00 a.m.–8:00 p.m.
Thurs–Fri; closed Sun
www.moor-mountain.com

Maynard Outdoor Store
24 Nason Street
Maynard, MA 01754
(978) 897-2133
Store hours: 9:00 a.m.–6:00 p.m. Mon–
Wed and Sat; 9:00 a.m.–9:00 p.m.
Thurs–Fri; noon–5:00 p.m. Sun

Natick Outdoor Store
38 North Avenue
Natick, MA 01760
(508) 653-9400
Store hours: 9:00 a.m.–6:00 p.m. Mon–
Wed and Sat; 9:00 a.m.–9:00 p.m.
Thurs–Fri; noon–5:00 p.m. Sun
www.natickoutdoor.com

New England Backpacker
6 East Mountain Street
Worcester, MA 01606
(508) 853-9407
Store hours: 10:00 a.m.–6:00 p.m.
Mon–Tues; 10:00 a.m.–8:00 p.m.
Wed–Fri; 10:00 a.m.–5:00 p.m. Sat;
noon–5:00 p.m. Sun
www.newenglandbackpacker.com

Eastern Mountain Sports–Boston
1041 Commonwealth Avenue
Boston, MA 02215
(617) 254-4250
Store hours: 10:00 a.m.–9:00 p.m.
Mon–Sat; noon–6:00 p.m. Sun
www.ems.com

Hike Index

About the Author

Steve Mirsky is an avid outdoorsman who has lived in New England for most of his life. He's hiked New Hampshire's Mount Washington in the winter, portions of the Long Trail in Vermont, and many a bend, overlook, and rock outcropping on trails throughout his home state of Connecticut. Steve has a special fondness for the Boston metropolitan area's diverse terrain and rich historical character.

Steve has over four years' experience as a freelance writer of destination features. He regularly covers food and culture on his blog at gastrotraveling.com and is also a regular contributor for http://magazine.istopover.com, covering the latest local news, restaurant reviews, and unique cultural offerings in New York City and across the world. Other articles have covered Brooklyn's "Boro Park," the country's largest Orthodox Jewish neighborhood, and "The International Express," a diverse conglomeration of neighborhoods in Queens, as well as Long Island's North Fork and the Hamptons.

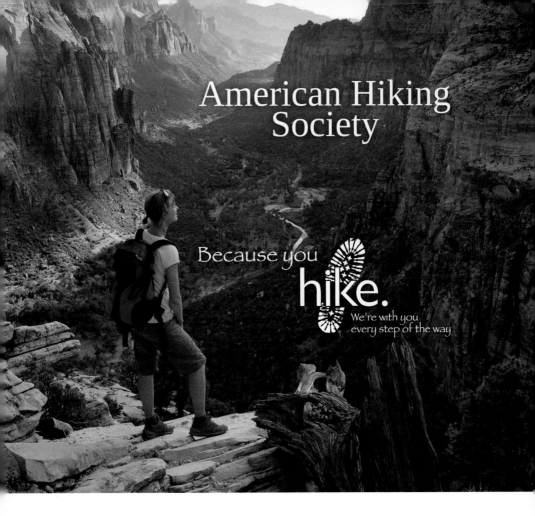

American Hiking Society

Because you hike.
We're with you every step of the way

As a national voice for hikers, **American Hiking Society** works every day:

- Building and maintaining hiking trails
- Educating and supporting hikers by providing information and resources
- Supporting hiking and trail organizations nationwide
- Speaking for hikers in the halls of Congress and with federal land managers

Whether you're a casual hiker or a seasoned backpacker, become a member of American Hiking Society and join the national hiking community! You'll enjoy great member benefits and help preserve the nation's hiking trails, so tomorrow's hike is even better than today's. We invite you to join us now!

American Hiking Society